"[*Depression 101*] is terrific. It comprehensively lays out several aspects of the education and self-help 'pearls' that I like to think I provide my own patients. This manual allows patients to participate actively in the management of their depression and provides patients with a pragmatic toolbox to help them 'fix' their depression and maintain health."

—Sidney Zisook, MD, professor of psychiatry and director of residency training at the University of California, San Diego School of Medicine

"I've been waiting for a book like this for a long time. *Depression 101* is the perfect book to recommend to friends, family, and clients who are struggling with depression. It's concise, easy to understand, and full of helpful information. It highlights the nature and causes of depression, the influences of sleep and caffeine, the most effective treatments available, and it provides several skills and strategies that the reader can use to combat the disorder. Whether you're buying this book for yourself or someone else, as an introduction to depression or as an adjunct to treatment, *Depression 101* will certainly be helpful in your recovery."

—Jeffrey C. Wood, Psy.D., clinical psychologist, author of *Getting Help*, and coauthor of *The Dialectical Behavior Therapy Skills Workbook*

DEPRESSION
101

A Practical Guide to

Treatments, Self-Help Strategies,
and Preventing Relapse

JOHN D. PRESTON, PSY.D., ABPP
MELISSA KIRK

New Harbinger Publications, Inc.

Publisher's Note

This publication is designed to provide accurate and authoritative information in regard to the subject matter covered. It is sold with the understanding that the publisher is not engaged in rendering psychological, financial, legal, or other professional services. If expert assistance or counseling is needed, the services of a competent professional should be sought.

Distributed in Canada by Raincoast Books

Copyright © 2010 by John D. Preston and Melissa Kirk
New Harbinger Publications, Inc.
5674 Shattuck Avenue
Oakland, CA 94609
www.newharbinger.com

All Rights Reserved
Printed in Canada

Acquired by Melissa Kirk
Cover design by Amy Shoup
Edited by Kayla Sussell

Library of Congress Cataloging-in-Publication Data on file with the publisher

12 11 10   10 9 8 7 6 5 4 3 2 1   First printing

Mixed Sources
Product group from well-managed forests, controlled sources and recycled wood or fibre
www.fsc.org Cert no. SW-COC-000952
© 1996 Forest Stewardship Council

This book is printed with soy ink.

To my students and psychotherapy patients...
you have been my best teachers.

—JP

To everyone who has ever struggled with depression.
May you find health, hope, and happiness.

—MK

Contents

Acknowledgments

I'd like to express my gratitude to Kayla Sussell for the many years of her excellent help in editing my books.

—John D. Preston

Thank you to everyone at New Harbinger, and to John Preston, for giving me the opportunity to work on this important book.

—Melissa Kirk

Introduction

Depression grabs you. It's stubborn, persistent, and relentless. Most people who experience depression try to snap out of it, ignore it, or at least endure it. But the nature of depression is to invade your life; it can rob you of vitality and demolish hope. No one has ever defeated depression simply by gritting his or her teeth or engaging in a "cheer yourself up" version of denial. One way or another, you will be moving through depression, but, clearly, there are ways to go about this that can reduce your suffering and promote recovery.

What works to combat depression are professional treatment and action-oriented self-help approaches. That's what this book is about. You are going to learn very specific action plans for helping yourself, and you can begin right now.

WHAT IS DEPRESSION?

Everyone has a down day once in a while; everyone has the blues now and then. Inevitably, disappointments, failures, and setbacks will be woven into the fabric of your life. And, sooner or later, each of us will experience very painful losses when friends or loved ones die. Unfortunately, this is a part of the price of membership in the human race.

But the experience of clinical depression is far beyond these common emotional elements of life. Serious depression is very common and one out of six of us will experience it (APA 2000).

However, there are fundamental differences between mild or temporary encounters with despair or sadness and clinical depression (often referred to as major depression or unipolar depression). Likewise, there are significant differences between normal grief and clinical depression. At first glance, these human experiences may seem similar, but upon closer inspection, the differences become clear.

Clinical depression is not just a feeling. It always is a cluster of symptoms, including, but not limited to, the following:

- Mood changes (sadness, intense irritability, feeling easily frustrated)

- Extremely negative thinking, including pessimism, a bleak view of the future, thoughts of hopelessness, fretting, worrying, brooding, and thoughts about suicide

- A loss of interest in most of life's activities; a profound lack of vitality

- Marked changes in physical functioning including sleep disturbances, fatigue and low energy, loss of sex drive, and changes in appetite and weight

You'll find a more extensive description of the symptoms of depression later in this chapter.

Clinical depression lasts a long time. If you are like most people who become depressed, you have done your best to overcome your depression, only to notice that you are quickly pulled back again into it again. The typical bout of major depression, if not treated, will last from six to fifteen months. After this prolonged period of suffering, about 75 percent of people will gradually come out of their depression (even without treatment); for the other 25 percent, it can hang on for months or years. Twenty percent of those who suffer with a severe depressive episode will, thankfully, never have another episode. But 80 percent of those with depression will reexperience depressive episodes or slip into chronic depression unless they receive appropriate treatment. For people with chronic or recurring depression, it is best to see depression as a form of chronic illness, similar to diabetes, high blood pressure, or asthma. The underlying disorder is always there, but people can experience remissions or control symptoms with ongoing treatment. Fortunately, with appropriate treatment, most people respond and recover (APA 2000; National Institute of Mental Health 2009).

UNDERSTANDING DEPRESSION

It is important to understand the distinctions between three human experiences: sadness, grief, and clinical depression.

Sadness

Sadness is considered a normal, healthy emotional reaction to minor losses and disappointments. Sadness is very transient, lasting only several minutes, a few hours, or, at most, a few days. It is unpleasant but typically doesn't interfere with your functioning. Normal, minor bouts of sadness don't knock you off your feet.

Grief

In contrast to sadness, grief is a much more intense and sometimes devastating human experience. However, it is considered an inevitable and normal emotional reaction that people in every culture across the world experience after a major loss, such as the death of a loved one or a divorce. Grief tends to have a major disruptive effect on the lives of the grief stricken and can result in prolonged periods of sadness, loneliness, and mourning, which can last anywhere from a few months to several years. We want to emphasize that normal grieving may last a very long time; broken hearts do not mend quickly. Grief is extremely painful, but it is not mental illness.

Grief also differs from depression in two other ways. With normal grief reactions, your feelings of self-esteem are generally unaffected. Despite great sadness, you continue to believe that you are a worthwhile individual. In clinical depression, feelings of worthlessness, inadequacy, and lack of self-confidence are common. Also, there are four symptoms of depression that are absent during times of grief: these are serious thoughts about suicide, severe sleep disturbances, marked agitation, and a complete loss of aliveness and vitality. This last point deserves some explanation.

Although the daily experience of a person grieving may be filled with feelings of loss and sadness, there is also the ability to experience moments of happiness. The grieving person may enjoy a funny movie, experience happiness when visiting a loved one, appreciate a nice meal, or enjoy seeing a beautiful landscape. Even while grieving, despite a good deal of suffering, thankfully, there can be times of pleasure and aliveness. Often, this is not the case with depression. With severe depression, most often there is no ability to experience even brief moments of happiness. Life feels boring, dull, and robbed of all vitality and meaningfulness.

Most people encountering major losses grieve but don't become seriously depressed and don't need psychological or psychiatric treatment. However, researchers have found that about 25 percent of those experiencing a major loss will, in fact, go on to develop depression and certainly may need and benefit from mental health treatment (Zisook 1993). In these cases, the depression must be resolved before people can begin to come to terms with their painful loss adequately. Treatment with medication may also be indicated when grief turns into depression.

■ Eleanor's Story

Eleanor is a sixty-eight-year-old widow. Four months ago her husband died of a stroke. The first weeks after his death she was consumed with grief and loss. The two had been husband and wife and each other's best friend for more than thirty-five years. All of her suffering made sense to her; she had lost her soul mate. However, two months after his death, Eleanor began to slip into a deep state of depression.

She began to experience a pervasive sense of fatigue and lethargy. Her sleep became fitful, and she began to awaken each morning at 4 a.m., unable to return to sleep. She became progressively withdrawn and felt cut off from life. She stopped attending church, which used to be a very important part of her life, and stopped answering the phone when it rang. She missed her husband terribly, but she was also sinking into the paralysis of depression. She felt worthless and believed that her life was no longer meaningful. Eleanor was experiencing what mental health professionals call *complicated bereavement*; that is, grief that has disintegrated into clinical depression.

Clinical Depression

Clinical depression is characterized by its intensity, duration, impact on functioning, and a host of specific symptoms. It is useful to consider two main sets of depressive symptoms: The first set is referred to as psychological symptoms, which are those symptoms seen in nearly all types of depression. The second group of symptoms are the biological or physical symptoms of depression.

PSYCHOLOGICAL SYMPTOMS OF DEPRESSION

The following list describes the symptoms common to all cases of depression:

- Feelings of sadness, despair, and emptiness

- Irritability

- A loss of interest in normal life activities

- Feeling bad about yourself combined with a lack of self-confidence

- Feeling apathetic and unmotivated, and not wanting to be around other people

- Feeling very emotionally sensitive

- Feeling negative and pessimistic

- Having thoughts about killing yourself

BIOLOGICAL SYMPTOMS OF DEPRESSION

This list details the biological changes that take place in severe depression:

- Changes in appetite—decreased or increased, with accompanying weight loss or weight gain

- Feeling very fatigued and slowed down

- Loss of sex drive

- Restlessness or agitation

- Difficulty concentrating

- Significant problems with sleep

There are several types of sleep disturbances common in depression: early morning awakening (for example waking up at

4 a.m. and being unable to return to sleep), frequent awakenings throughout the night, and excessive sleeping. Note that difficulty in falling asleep may be seen with depression, but this can be seen with anyone experiencing stress in general.

Not all depressed people will have all of these symptoms, but if you are experiencing several of them, there's a good chance you are depressed and should see a physician or mental health professional to receive an evaluation. Generally, for a diagnosis of depression to be made, such symptoms must be present for a period lasting at least two weeks (APA 2000).

WEEKLY DEPRESSION RATING SCALE

To see if you might be clinically depressed, please read through the following list and rate how frequently you've experienced each symptom over the past week by placing a check mark in the appropriate column.

ARE YOU DEPRESSED?

During the past week	None or a little of the time (0-2 days)	Some of the time (3-5 days)	Most of the time (6-7 days)
Waking up at night or in the early morning, unable to return to sleep			
Very restless sleep			

Loss of energy; fatigue			
Decreased sex drive			
Unable to enjoy life; loss of zest for life			
Withdrawing from others			
Strong thoughts of suicide			
Loss of appetite			
Memory problems, forgetfulness, or poor concentration			
Feeling irritable or easily frustrated			
Feelings of sadness, hopelessness, or unhappiness			
Sleeping a lot			
Feelings of low self-esteem			
Apathy or low motivation			

If you've checked more than five of the items in the "Some of the Time" or "Most of Time" columns, you may be struggling with clinical depression and, would probably be helped by seeking a diagnosis from a health care professional. In the meantime, keep reading this book to discover ways to experience relief from your symptoms.

BIPOLAR DISORDER

Serious depression comes in two varieties: unipolar and bipolar. When you have bipolar disorder, you experience both depression and episodes of *mania* (extreme states of agitation, hyperactivity, euphoria, marked irritability, decreased need for sleep, racing thoughts, and sometimes psychotic symptoms) or *hypomania* (milder episodes of increased energy, euphoric mood, and decreased need for sleep). *Unipolar depression* involves only depressive episodes, never mania or hypomania.

For the majority of people suffering from bipolar disorder, their first mood episode is serious depression (Goodwin and Jamison 2007). If this were the case for you, you wouldn't necessarily know right away that you had bipolar disorder rather than unipolar depression.

Unfortunately, antidepressant medications are risky drugs to use for treating bipolar depression, since they can cause a depressed person to switch from a state of depression to mania, and over time the drugs can worsen the course of bipolar disorder. For that reason, it's important for you to get the right diagnosis so you can receive appropriate treatment. If you have experienced the following, you may be at a higher risk for bipolar disorder:

■ Depressive symptoms that include hypersomnia (excessive sleeping), increased appetite, and weight gain.

- Depression that hasn't responded to antidepressant medication treatments

- Psychotic symptoms (for example, delusions or hallucinations)

- Having blood relatives who have had bipolar disorder

If you are suffering from depression, it's very important that you be screened for possible bipolar disorder. The list above is helpful, and we also strongly recommend that you take the self-administered Mood Disorder Questionnaire, which can be found on the following website: http://www.dbsalliance.org/pdfs/MDQ.pdf. Please share the results from this test with your therapist or physician.

THE CAUSES OF DEPRESSION

Depression can be caused by many factors. Most of the time, it's a reaction to stressful life experiences, such as the loss of a loved one to death or divorce, the loss of a job, ongoing and severe familial stresses, and so forth. In addition to normal life stresses, certain biological changes can also trigger depression. These include a number of physical diseases. Some medical conditions change body chemistry and ultimately affect the delicate chemical balance of the brain. For this reason we strongly recommend that you see your physician and have a complete physical exam and basic lab tests to determine whether there are any medical conditions present that may be causing your depression. (See appendix A at the back of the book.)

If a particular physical illness is causing your depression, then the approach of choice, generally, is to focus on treating the particular disease (for example, thyroid disease). When the disorder has been successfully treated, depressive symptoms typically subside. In other cases antidepressant medication and psychotherapy may play an important role as part of the total treatment package. Moreover, a number of medications and recreational drugs (for example, alcohol) may cause depression. Drugs that may cause depression are listed in appendix B.

TREATMENT IS ESSENTIAL

In the United States, it is estimated that two-thirds of people suffering from clinical depression never receive treatment (Young et al. 2001). This is especially disturbing since most depressions can usually be treated successfully. Left untreated, people suffer tremendously and needlessly. Lives are ruined, marriages fall apart, school performance plummets, jobs are lost, health can become compromised, and many people turn to increased alcohol use (and abuse), and some commit suicide.

This need not happen. The keys to avoiding such negative results are these:

- Take action to get professional help, which includes psychotherapy and perhaps treatment with antidepressant medications.

- Learn about depression and make sure that family members learn about it as well. During recovery from depression, ongoing support from family members can be crucial, but for this to occur, family members must become well-informed about depression.

■ Develop an attitude of compassion for yourself. This is critical. Stem the tide of harsh self-criticism, and be kind to yourself.

■ Finally (and this takes us to the purpose of this book), adopting an action-oriented strategy that pulls out all of the stops, using a number of self-help approaches that have proved to be powerful methods for reducing depression, can be enormously helpful while you are combating depression.

A Note to Friends or Loved Ones

If you are reading this book because of concern for a close friend or family member, please keep in mind that the nature of depression is to withdraw and to experience helplessness, pessimism, and/or powerlessness. Almost half of people in the United States who experience serious depression never seek treatment. Normal attempts to encourage or cheer up a person who is in the throes of clinical depression almost always fail. The most important thing you can do is to speak to your friend or family member in a frank and compassionate way. After listening, let your loved one know that you understand about the nature of depression (hopefully this book will be helpful in understanding the experience) and let the person know you are very concerned and that you feel compelled to help him or her seek professional treatment.

This book is loaded with self-help strategies that often are successful in battling depression, but with severe depressions, professional help is *always* necessary. If your friend or family member minimizes his or her plight or seems reluctant to pursue getting professional help, please be persistent in encouraging the person to seek help. And if your loved one seems too immobilized by the depression or is in other ways unable to initiate treatment on his or her own, it is often very helpful for others to offer assistance in making a first appointment with a therapist or physician. You might say, "I cannot in good conscience be silent about this. I know you are seriously depressed. I know many people with depression just feel like giving up, and I also know most people who seek treatment recover. Please let me help you make a first appointment with a therapist. I'm doing this because I am concerned and because I love you. I believe that you would do the same for me if I were in your shoes."

GETTING STARTED

As noted psychiatrist David Burns frequently says, depression may feel hopeless, but treatments for depression are generally very effective (1999). The major roadblock to overcoming depression is depression itself: the feelings of pessimism that are a hallmark of depression lead many sufferers to stop dead in their tracks and conclude, "Nothing can help me." Action is the antidote for powerlessness. All of the strategies outlined in this book are strongly supported in research as being effective in treating depression. However, we need to be realistic and honest about this. Often self-help strategies are not possible if a person is too debilitated by depression. We sincerely believe that this book will be helpful in your recovery from depression. At the same time, if you find that you are unable to get started with the approaches outlined in this book, there are two practical choices you can make. You can enlist the help of a close friend or family member to help you get started on and follow through with the treatment suggestions. Or, you can make what may be a lifesaving decision to seek professional treatment. We will discuss seeking professional treatment and offer suggestions about how to go about doing this in a subsequent chapter. For many people, self-help approaches are only doable once they have received some improvement from professional treatment. The first chapter will begin to outline action plans that you can use, starting today, to fight back against depression and to regain your life.

CHAPTER ONE

The Challenge of Depression

When you have depression, you may feel so low that you can never imagine getting out from under the blackness of your mood. Every decision may seem both monumental and pointless, and on top of that, there are so many books, websites, advertisements, talk shows, and advice columns out there, all telling you the best way to treat your depression, that the information overload may seem confusing and overwhelming. Television commercials say the best way to feel better is to take a pill and make the pain go away; the thick workbooks at the bookstore all promise a quick cure using their particular treatment method; therapists use a confusing alphabet soup of acronyms, and each seems to offer a different type of therapy; and the health-food stores offer shelves and shelves of supplements, herbs, and pills that all say they can help heal depression.

You've also heard that exercise, yoga, meditation, and hypnosis can help. Your friends and family may be telling you to just snap out of it, that you just need to try harder, or that things really aren't that bad. You may even feel as if there's no way to sort through the confusion to find the best treatment for yourself. But there is a way. In this chapter, we'll provide a short overview of the treatments that have been found to be the most effective for treating depression.

GETTING A DIAGNOSIS

With depression, the most important first step is to get an accurate diagnosis. Note that certain physical health conditions can cause feelings of sadness, lethargy, and lack of motivation, so it's important to first make sure that what you're experiencing is, in fact, depression. For example, in the introduction, we discussed how depression differs from other disorders, such as bipolar disorder. Regardless of what's going on, if you're feeling so down that you picked up this book, most likely you would benefit from seeing a health practitioner as your first step toward feeling better.

Several practitioners can diagnose depression. If you have a medical doctor you see regularly, he or she can rule out any medical conditions and can screen you for depression or other common mental health issues. Since depression is so common, many general practitioners and family practice doctors now screen patients for depression as a normal part of any health checkup. Your doctor can then give you a referral to a psychotherapist or support group and to other resources you can go to for help. You can also seek out a psychiatrist, who can prescribe medications for your depression if you both decide that's the best option. A clinical psychologist or licensed therapist is also qualified to make a diagnosis of depression. All of these health care professionals can then help you decide the best way to begin treatment.

SEEKING TREATMENT

Once you're sure you have clinical depression and not another disorder or a physiological problem, the next step is to decide which treatment is the best option for you. With depression, the best way to get better is to seek more than one type of treatment and to combine treatment with lifestyle changes, such as getting enough sleep and exercise, eating right, and dealing with issues that may be linked to depression, such as substance abuse. You may decide to take an antidepressant as well as to find a therapist to teach you better coping skills. Or you may decide to try Saint-John's-wort and a fish-oil supplement, join a yoga class, or join a support group especially for people with depression. Every person with depression will have a different path to mental wellness, so you'll need to be persistent in exploring your options until you find a combination that works well for you. If something doesn't seem to be working, it's okay to try something else instead, as long as you give the first method a chance to work. We'll discuss proven treatment methods in the following pages.

MEDICATIONS

There are many different types of antidepressants on the market. If you decide to use prescription medication, it's important that you work with your medical provider to find the right medication, or combination of medications, and the right dosage for yourself. Report any symptoms or troubling side effects in detail to your medical provider, and be aware that most antidepressants can take between two to six weeks to work. Also bear in mind that about 25 percent of those who ultimately have a good response to antidepressants require eight to ten weeks of treatment before their symptoms go away (Preston, O'Neal, and Talaga 2010). If you don't immediately feel better, be sure that you've given the medication enough time to have an effect.

It's also important to never stop taking your medications suddenly, as this may cause withdrawal symptoms or trigger the return of a depressive episode. Always work with your health care provider to decide when and how to discontinue your medications. The most commonly used types of antidepressant medications are described below.

Prescription Medications

Whether or not to use antidepressant medications is perhaps the most controversial aspect of depressive illness. Almost every day there's a story in the popular media about the dangers of antidepressants or a report of yet another research study that questions the efficacy of a particular antidepressant. And even though antidepressant use is soaring in the United States, there is still a stigma about admitting you're taking them. In spite of the stigma, antidepressants can and do work for most people with depression. With proper treatment, antidepressants are effective for about 70 percent of those treated—even those with serious depressions. They can be a lifesaving first step in stabilizing mood, especially when your depression has affected your functioning to the extent that you are in danger of losing your job or an important relationship, or you are at risk of harming yourself (Agency for Health Care Policy and Research 1999).

Selective serotonin reuptake inhibitors (SSRIs). These are the most commonly prescribed antidepressants because they have been proven effective and safe for most people. SSRIs work by increasing the availability of the neurotransmitter serotonin in the brain. Common SSRIs include Lexapro (escitalopram), Celexa (citalopram), Prozac (fluoxetine), Paxil (paroxetine), and Zoloft (sertraline). Common side effects of SSRIs include nausea, headaches, fatigue, and sexual dysfunction. Please note that sexual side effects with antidepressants occur in about 14 to 39 percent of people being treated (Clayton et al. 2002). The specific side effect is *inorgasmia* (difficulty achieving an orgasm). Impotency is very rare.

Serotonin and norepinephrine reuptake inhibitors (SNRIs). This class of drugs is relatively new, and they work by increasing the availability of both serotonin and norepinephrine. SNRIs include Cymbalta (duloxetine), Effexor (venlafaxine), and Pristiq (desvenlafaxine). Side effects can include nausea, anxiety, fatigue, and sexual dysfunction.

Atypical antidepressants. Atypical antidepressants include Wellbutrin (bupropion), which works by increasing levels of the neurotransmitters norepinephrine and dopamine, and Remeron (mirtazapine), which increases levels of serotonin and norepinephrine. The side effects of Wellbutrin can include irritability, headaches, insomnia, and stomach upset, although the sexual problems and weight gain found with other antidepressants occur less frequently with this drug. The side effects of Remeron may include weight gain, an increased appetite, sleepiness, and dizziness.

Tricyclic antidepressants (TCAs). These drugs are often used when other classes of antidepressants have been tried without success. They work by increasing the available levels of serotonin or norepinephrine, but they can have significant side effects and drug interactions, and it is possible to overdose on them. TCAs include Elavil (amitriptyline), Tofranil (imipramine), Pamelor (nortriptyline), Norpramin (desipramine), and Anafranil (clomipramine). Common side effects include sedation, dry mouth, blurry vision, constipation, urination problems, rapid heartbeat, and light-headedness.

Monoamine oxidase inhibitors (MAOIs). These medications were developed in the mid-1950s and include some of the earliest drugs used to treat depression. This class of drugs is most often used for depression that doesn't respond to the other types of drugs; they work by blocking the enzyme monoamine oxidase from breaking down neurochemicals in the brain that are responsible for mood changes. These drugs include Nardil (phenelzine), Parnate (tranylcypromine), Emsam (selegiline), and Marplan (isocarboxazid). MAOIs are not commonly prescribed because they can have serious interactions with foods such as red wine, chocolate, cheese, and certain meats that contain the compound tyramine (for example, bologna, salami, and Spam). However, MAOIs are often effective treatments for difficult-to-treat depression.

Over-the-Counter Medications

There are several over-the-counter treatments for depression that have been found to be helpful for moderate depression, although not usually for severe depression. If your depression is mild to moderate, you might consider trying these over-the-counter products, along with the lifestyle tips included in this book, before you seek a prescription for antidepressant medications.

Saint-John's-wort. This herb has been used for medicinal purposes in naturopathic medicine. In clinical trials it has been shown to be effective for mild to moderate depression (Linde et al. 2009) in dosages between 900 to 1,800 mg a day. Saint-John's-wort has few side effects and is well tolerated, but it can cause significant and sometimes dangerous interactions with some prescription medications. Saint-John's-wort can take three to six weeks to work, and there's some concern that it may have significant negative interactions with prescription antidepressant medications. If you choose to take Saint-John's-wort, be sure to let your health care provider know, especially if you are taking or considering taking prescription medications.

S-adenosylmethionine (SAM-e). SAM-e has been shown to be effective for mild to moderate depression, when compared to a placebo (Lu 2000; Papakostas, Alpert, and Fava 2003), in dosages of 400 to 1,600 mg a day, and, so far, no significant drug interactions or side effects have been discovered. However, you should be cautious in using SAM-e if you have anxiety, low blood sugar, or diabetes. SAM-e has been shown to cause mania in people who suffer from bipolar disorder. Moreover, SAM-e should always be taken with a vitamin B complex supplement.

Omega-3 fatty acids. Omega-3s are found in cold-water fish and certain nuts and vegetables. They can also be bought over the counter in liquid or capsule form at health-food stores and well-stocked supermarkets. Omega-3s can have a positive effect on mood in doses as low as 1 gram per day and have no known side effects (Peet and Horrobin 2002; Su et al. 2008).

5-hydroxytryptophan (5-HTP). This supplement may be effective for mild to moderate depression in doses of 300 mg per day (Poldinger, Calancini, and Schwartz 1991).

PSYCHOTHERAPY

In some studies, talk therapy has been shown to be as effective as antidepressants (DeRubeis et al. 2005), and frequently the combination of psychotherapy and antidepressants has been found to be the most effective treatment for depression, especially severe depression (Pampallona et al. 2004). Depression is often caused by a combination of chemical imbalances in the brain and life circumstances, including highly stressful life events, unhealthy thought patterns, and maladaptive coping patterns.

Although antidepressants can help the neurochemical imbalance, they can't help you learn new ways to think or new ways to approach life's problems. A qualified therapist can help you learn better coping skills that can, in turn, help you feel better about your life. Here are several types of therapy most often recommended for the treatment of depression.

Cognitive Behavioral Therapy (CBT)

CBT is the most well-researched and most commonly prescribed type of therapy used to treat depression. The concept behind CBT is that when you're depressed, your thinking patterns are skewed. You tend to dwell on negative events, overgeneralize about normal problems, see matters only in black and white, anticipate negative outcomes, assume the worst about others' intentions, and set unfair or unrealistic standards for yourself and others. As you can imagine, these types of thoughts can make a depressed person's inner world a very unfriendly and negative place. CBT aims to teach the depressed person new ways to think that are more balanced and realistic, and then to change certain behaviors that may be contributing to the depression.

For example, when something difficult happens, many depressed people assume that their friends won't want to hear about it, so they isolate themselves rather than reach out for support. A CBT therapist might first help depressed clients to critically examine their thoughts about their friends not wanting to hear about their problems. Following that review, the therapist would then help depressed people to change their pattern of isolating themselves, encouraging them to call a trusted friend when they feel sad or upset instead of keeping to themselves. In this way, CBT helps depressed people engage in activities that are more likely to help them feel better, such as connecting with a social support network, learning to look at the big picture rather than focusing on smaller, negative events, and developing compassion for themselves and others. You'll find a discussion of the specific techniques of CBT in chapter 3.

Acceptance and Commitment Therapy (ACT)

ACT is a relatively recent form of therapy that combines behavioral therapy with mindfulness and personal values work. ACT therapists believe that one reason people feel depressed is that they become so entangled with their stories about themselves (for example, "I'm a failure," "I'm a loser," "I'm too fat," or "I'm too shy to make friends") that they lose track of their personal values and life goals.

In addition, ACT practitioners believe that suffering is caused by our human tendency to fight against feeling uncomfortable emotions and experiences, and that these struggles, which also knock us off track in our lives, can be a source of significant stress. For example, someone who feels that she is unattractive might say to herself, "I'm too plain to meet anyone who will want to be in a relationship with me," and as she struggles with this difficult belief, she becomes depressed. An ACT therapist might help her learn to accept her anxiety about her attractiveness, understand that this is just a feeling and not an absolute truth, and encourage her to go out and socialize anyway, as a way to live in accord with the value she gives to being socially connected and active.

ACT also uses meditation and mindfulness techniques to help people stay in the moment with their life experiences, rather than spin off into negative or unhelpful stories about what's happening, why it's happening, what the event means about them, and so forth.

Dialectical Behavior Therapy (DBT)

DBT is a treatment designed to help those who have trouble regulating their emotions. Originally developed for the treatment of borderline personality disorder, DBT has also shown promise in treating depression. The major goal of DBT is to minimize or eliminate self-harming behaviors by teaching people the skills needed to tolerate the emotional discomfort that causes them to turn to self-harm or, in a worst-case scenario, suicide.

A DBT practitioner will teach you how to accept contradictory thoughts at the same time—specifically, how to accept yourself with all of your problems and issues while also understanding that you will need to change some of your behaviors and thought patterns to function in healthier ways. As in ACT, DBT practitioners teach mindfulness skills to help people observe their thoughts, actions, and emotions without judging or reacting to them in harmful ways. Skills for coping with overwhelming emotions are discussed in chapter 5.

Interpersonal Therapy (IPT)

This form of therapy focuses on how people interact with others. Many people who are depressed have trouble interacting with the people around them in healthy, positive ways. For example, you may have trouble engaging with others, may tend to focus on the negative, or may feel so sad that your body language, facial expression, and tone of voice make others uncomfortable. Often, people with depression feel socially isolated, and if you are unaware of how you interact with others, you may end up pushing people away, when what you really need is to feel more socially engaged and accepted.

IPT's aim is to help people explore their important relationships, understand how their depression may be affecting their relationships, and, in turn, explore how interpersonal issues may be affecting their emotional state. We explore more about interpersonal skills in chapter 6.

Behavioral Therapy

Social withdrawal and isolation are very common symptoms of depression. Additionally, most people suffering from depression become quite sedentary, which can increase and prolong depression. Behavior therapists use techniques that target both social withdrawal and decreased physical activity, helping to mobilize people to stay engaged with life. At first glance, such an approach may seem simplistic, yet some experts think behavior therapy is one of the most effective treatments for depression (Flora 2007).

Talk Therapy

Common experiences that can lead to depression include the experience of loss (the death of a loved one or a divorce), major disappointments (for example, being fired from a job or rejected in a relationship or having ongoing, serious relationship problems), and encounters with trauma and tragedy (for example, having a child diagnosed with a serious illness or having been raped). Clearly, many people in the throes of such difficult life circumstances often grit their teeth and try to push ahead with their lives.

This strategy works for some, but it is not uncommon that bottling up feelings, in and of itself, can backfire and result in depression. Such people live with unresolved grief or a good deal of internal turmoil and conflict. Talk therapy, which, as its name suggests, simply means giving voice to your feelings and experiences in a safe place, can help you to openly explore and resolve your inner suffering. It can be tremendously helpful for many people suffering from depression. This is especially so if you've been encountering very difficult life circumstances, such as the loss of a loved one or another major life transition.

Finding a Therapist

Finding the right therapist for yourself won't be as easy as stopping at the supermarket to pick up a loaf of bread. You may need to talk to several therapists to find someone who is a good match for you in temperament, treatment method, cost, and location. Moreover, as in any relationship, the chemistry between the two of you must be right if you are to work well together.

If one of the treatments mentioned above sounds like something you'd like to try, you're off to a head start, because you can look for a therapist who offers that type of therapy. Most therapists will use different methods for different issues, but if you feel strongly about a particular approach, finding someone who specializes in that technique will be your first order of business.

To find therapists in your area, consider the following ways:

■ Ask for a referral from your primary care provider.

■ Search the Internet or your local phone book for mental health agencies in your area, and ask them for a list of treatment providers. If the organization has a website, you may be able to type in your zip code and get a list of practitioners near your home or your job.

■ Look at ads for therapists in local publications, such as newspapers and local-interest magazines, and contact the ones who appeal to you.

■ You can get online referrals from the American Psychological Association at http:/locator.apa.org or Psych Central at http://therapists.psychcentral.com.

■ If you have a trusted friend or family member who has been in therapy and was satisfied with his or her therapist, consider contacting that therapist.

WHAT TO ASK

Once you have some phone numbers, call the therapists and let them know you are seeking treatment for depression. Most therapists will be able to speak to you for a few minutes to answer some common questions, and to get a sense of what you are looking for. Some questions you might want to ask a potential therapist are these:

- Do you have experience treating depression?

- What is your primary treatment method? (If you know what type of therapeutic method you're looking for, let the therapist know that, and ask if he or she has experience with using that type of treatment.)

- How much will the treatment cost?

- Do you accept my type of insurance?

- If you feel that it is indicated, do you treat patients with depression with antidepressant medications or make a referral for such treatment?

- What medical tests do you recommend for depressed patients? [*Note:* This should include a general medical exam, standard lab tests and in particular thyroid screening, because about 10 percent of people with depression have thyroid disease, either obvious or subtle, and competent therapists should know this. If no medical tests are recommended, this person may not be a seasoned therapist, in terms of comprehensive treatment for depression.]

- In your experience, when you have treated depressed patients and they have had little or no response to treatment, what are your *specific* strategies and further treatment recommendations? [Note: This final question is a good one to determine if a potential therapist truly knows about the treatment of depression. This question really explores the experience and competence of the therapist. The fact is that about 33 percent of people seeking treatment for depression have very good outcomes from standardized treatments (psychotherapy and/or a trial on antidepressant medications). The other two-thirds of patients often do respond to treatments, but need more aggressive and combination treatments, such as systematic trials on various antidepressants or combination medication treatments, or adjunctive treatments such as exercise, bright light therapy, and psychotherapy.]

DECIDING ON A THERAPIST

You are the only one who knows whether or not you will be able to work with a particular therapist. During your first phone call or your initial session, if you feel uncomfortable with the therapist's demeanor, personality, or approach, it's in your best interests to bring this up immediately with the therapist. Your discomfort might be a sign that the therapist is ready to challenge you to change for the better. On the other hand, it might be a sign that you will be unable to relax and let down your guard with the person, which may impede your treatment. If you believe that it might be difficult to work with him or her, it's okay if you decide not to see that particular therapist.

Making Long-Term Changes

In this chapter, we've discussed the first-line treatments for clinical depression. It's not absolutely necessary for you to take prescription medications or over-the-counter supplements, or to begin a course of therapy. But if you're feeling so awful that you have a difficult time functioning, these approaches can help you start to gain control of your depression so that you'll have the energy and motivation to make substantive, long-term changes.

If you've decided, for the moment, not to seek medication or therapy, you might find that the techniques in this book are both helpful and useful as you continue on your quest to heal from depression and to enjoy life again.

A NOTE ON SUICIDAL THOUGHTS AND SELF-HARM

Before we get started, here is some straight and sober talk about suicide. Beyond the tremendous suffering that depression can cause, 9 percent of people plagued by depression take their own lives. It's likely that the *majority* of people experiencing depression may have *some* thoughts about suicide or other forms of self-harm. Most never actually plan a suicide attempt. Thoughts of suicide stem from significant feelings of pessimism and hopelessness or from anger and frustration at oneself or others. Also, it is worth noting that suicide is more likely in those who are depressed and also using alcohol or illicit drugs. Any time a person has thoughts of suicide, this should be taken very seriously. If you are having thoughts about suicide or self-harm, it is very important for you to speak to someone about this. Certainly it is important and appropriate to share your feelings with a close friend, clergy, or a loved one. And it is essential that you contact your physician or seek treatment from a qualified psychotherapist. Please do not feel afraid to talk to a professional about these concerns. Once again, most depressed people who have thoughts of suicide do not actually attempt suicide, but it is a warning signal that you are feeling desperate or hopeless. This is the time to reach out. If you are reading this book because of your concern about a friend or loved one, when suicidal thoughts are expressed, do not hesitate to contact a mental health professional and enlist help in getting treatment for your loved one. Another resource is to call 1-800-SUICIDE.

CHAPTER TWO

Lifestyle Choices to Improve Depression

Sometimes the very lifestyle choices that can improve depression are exactly the things that are the hardest to do when you're depressed. Getting enough restful sleep, eating right, and getting enough exercise can improve depressive symptoms, but when you're depressed, you may find that you have trouble sleeping, you either lose your appetite or eat too much, or you have a difficult time staying motivated to exercise.

In this chapter, we'll discuss ways you can make improvements in all three of these areas, as well as ways to help yourself stay sufficiently motivated to continue making healthy lifestyle choices.

THE IMPORTANCE OF SLEEP

Disordered sleep is extremely common in people with depression. Insomnia is especially common, particularly waking frequently throughout the night and waking early in the morning and being unable to return to sleep. Even if they do manage to sleep through the night, people with depression may also have poor quality sleep. This means that you don't get enough deep, restful sleep, which can result in fatigue during the day, forgetfulness, an inability to concentrate, and heightened emotional sensitivity, such as being more easily frustrated and overwhelmed. Long-term insomnia may even be at the root of some cases of depression (Ford and Kamerow 1989; Goodwin and Jamison 2007).

Good Sleep Hygiene

It may seem counterintuitive to have to work at getting a good night's sleep, but sleep experts have found that good sleep habits, otherwise known as sleep hygiene, can improve your likelihood of enjoying healthy sleep. If you have trouble sleeping, here are some simple ways to improve your sleep hygiene.

Stick to a sleep schedule. Go to bed at the same time every night and get up at the same time every morning, even on weekends. Sticking to a schedule helps to reset your body's internal clock.

Use your bed only for sleeping and sexual activity. Don't read, watch TV, pay bills, or do anything in your bed except sleeping and having sex. This allows your body and brain to understand that the bed is there for sleep and relaxation, so when you climb into bed, you're already primed to fall asleep.

Don't lie awake in bed for longer than twenty minutes. If you can't fall asleep within twenty minutes, get up and do something relaxing before trying again. Read a calming book, meditate, or do a relaxation exercise, and then when you feel sleepy, go back to bed.

Decrease your caffeine intake. Many people with sleep difficulties use caffeine to stay alert during the day, but caffeine can disrupt sleep even if you have only one cup of coffee in the morning. If you have trouble sleeping, try cutting back or avoiding caffeine altogether for a week to see if your sleep improves. Remember that coffee isn't the only thing that contains caffeine; soda, some teas, chocolate, and some over-the-counter and prescription medications also contain caffeine. Antidepressant medication can also increase the time caffeine stays in your bloodstream, so if you're on antidepressants and are still experiencing insomnia, it may be helpful to limit your intake of any type of caffeine. It's important to keep your daily caffeine intake to 250 mg or less, and to consume caffeine only before noon. It's easy to determine your caffeine consumption if you consult the following chart, which provides the caffeine content of many popular beverages and a candy bar.

Caffeine Content of Common Substances*

Beverages and Candy	oz	mg	Over-the-Counter Drugs**	mg
Caffeinated soft drinks	12	40-60	Anacin	32
Chocolate candy bar	1.55	10	Appetite-control pills	100-200
Coffee	6	125	Dristan	16
Decaf coffee	6	5	Excedrin	65
Energy drinks	12	250	Extra Strength Excedrin	100
Espresso	1	50	Midol	132
Green tea	6	30	No Doz	100
Hot cocoa	6	15	Triaminicin	30
Black tea	6	50	Vanquish	33
Prescription Drugs			Vivarin	200
Cafergot		100		
Darvan Compound		32		
Fiorinal		40		

Total mg caffeine per day _____

*Source: FDA National Center: Drugs and Biologics (as cited in Avis 1993)
**Per Tablet

Reduce heavy use of caffeine gradually. If you are using amounts of caffeine that exceed 750 mg per day, you'll need to gradually reduce your daily consumption in order to prevent caffeine withdrawal, which causes symptoms of headache, jitteriness, and, interestingly, insomnia. You can withdraw gradually by reducing your caffeine intake by 25 percent the first week and by a similar amount each week thereafter. For example, if you're consuming 1,000 mg of caffeine per day, the first week your goal would be to cut back to 750 mg per day. The next week, decrease it to 500 mg per day, and so forth. If you experience symptoms of caffeine withdrawal, then reduce your rate of discontinuation; for example, by 100 mg per week. Most people with depression imagine that this approach is unlikely to make a difference, but it's a very useful strategy that improves the quality of sleep and helps to reduce depression.

Create a comfortable sleep environment. A cool bedroom is more conducive to sleep than a warm one. A room temperature between 65 and 68 degrees is ideal. Keep extra blankets on the bed if you tend to get cold. Consider investing in blinds or curtains that shut out most outside light. If you find that your bedroom is too noisy or your bed partner snores, try earplugs and a white noise machine or a CD of calming sounds, such as ocean waves breaking on a beach. Consider using aromatherapy to enhance the sense of calmness in your bedroom. Try lavender, sandalwood, Roman chamomile, or clary sage to induce restful sleep. This may sound like pop psychology, but there is evidence that these approaches often work; the part of the brain that processes the sense of smell also plays a role in emotions.

You might even consider removing anything that makes you feel stressed or anxious from your bedroom, such as the desk where you pay bills, the computer where you write reports for work, or photographs or other items that remind you of someone with whom you have a troubled relationship. Your bedroom should be a place where you feel safe, calm, and comfortable.

Avoid nicotine, alcohol, and heavy meals close to bedtime. Nicotine is a stimulant that can cause disrupted sleep. Alcohol, though sedating, tends to wear off in the middle of the night, causing early morning waking. Stick to relaxing caffeine-free tea. Heavy meals can cause indigestion and discomfort that may also disrupt sleep.

Avoid strenuous exercise right before bedtime. If you must exercise close to your bedtime, try low-impact stretches or a calming yoga routine instead of a vigorous workout.

Establish a regular, relaxing nighttime ritual. By doing the same calming ritual before going to bed every night, you signal to your body that you're about to sleep. Meditate for ten minutes, read a relaxing book, do breathing or relaxation exercises, write in a gratitude journal, or spend some relaxing time with a pet or partner. Do anything that calms you in preparation for a good night's sleep.

Shutting Down Your Brain

Quite often, people with depression find that one reason they can't fall asleep is that their brain just won't stop running. Some people use the metaphor of a hamster running constantly on a wheel and getting nowhere, without ever showing any sign of stopping. You may find yourself preoccupied with worries, ruminating about a stressful event that occurred earlier that day, plagued by regrets about your past, or haunted by self-critical thoughts. Here are a few simple techniques that may help you to calm restless thoughts that keep you awake.

EYE MOVEMENT EXERCISE

It may seem strange, but back-and-forth eye movements have been shown to be effective in shutting off or calming the brain's stress response; they do this by activating the *parasympathetic nervous system*. This is the part of the nervous system that, when stimulated, slows heart rate, lowers blood pressure, and slows breathing. This exercise takes about two minutes.

Step 1. If you wear contact lenses, remove them. Sit comfortably in a chair and take a minute to relax and become calm.

Step 2. Once you feel centered, begin to move your eyes back and forth while keeping your head and neck still, as if you were watching the ball in a tennis game. Keep your eyes open, and take about one second each time to shift your eyes from right to left and back again.

Step 3. Repeat this eye movement about twenty times; then stop, close your eyes, and relax.

Step 4. Keeping your eyes closed, scan your body and become aware of any tension or discomfort in any part of your body. Simply notice any tension you feel.

Step 5. Repeat step 2, and after twenty repetitions, close your eyes and relax for a few seconds, then repeat the eye movements a third time. You should feel calmer and able to observe that your mental activity has slowed.

Once you get the hang of doing these steps, try doing them when you first get into bed every night, repeating steps 3 through 5 two or three times.

PROGRESSIVE MUSCLE RELAXATION

Another technique for calming the mind involves calming the body. This exercise can be done in bed when you retire, but you can also do it sitting in a chair or lying on a sofa or on the floor.

To begin, get as relaxed as you can while reclining or sitting. Feel the pull of gravity on your muscles. Close your eyes and take two deep, slow breaths. Exhale slowly and, as you exhale, notice the tension leaving your body. After a few seconds, begin the progressive muscle relaxation by tensing each of the following muscle groups in sequence. Hold the tension in each area for a count of 3, and then release it. Pay special attention to the sensation of release each time you relax your muscles. Pause for ten to fifteen seconds between muscle groups. Tense and release your muscle groups in the following order:

1. Feet and toes

2. Calves and lower legs

3. Thighs

4. Buttocks (squeeze them together)

5. Abdomen

6. Lower back (arch your back gently)

7. Chest (take a deep breath and hold it)

8. Hands (make fists)

9. Upper arms

10. Shoulders (shrug your shoulders up toward your ears and hold)

11. Face (squeeze your eyes closed, purse your lips, and hold)

12. Face (open your eyes and mouth as wide as you can, then hold)

It may help to go through this sequence twice a day for ten to fifteen minutes each time as you familiarize yourself with the exercise, especially if you notice yourself experiencing a lot of physical tension during your day. You'll find that as you become more familiar with doing it, you'll reduce the time you spend doing the exercise to four to five minutes, instead of the ten to fifteen minutes needed to do when you first start.

CONTROLLED BREATHING

Here's a simple breathing technique that activates the parasympathetic nervous system and helps to induce relaxation. Take a deep breath, counting to 4 as you inhale. Hold for a count of 6, then slowly exhale for a count of 8. Repeat five times.

NUTRITION AND MOOD

Often people with depression don't eat very well. You might find yourself snacking mostly on junk food or foods high in carbohydrates or fat, and you might find that you don't feel motivated to shop and cook healthy foods. Since foods high in carbohydrates often provide a temporary elevation in mood, many depressed people choose these foods as a way to try to feel better. Some people with depression stop eating much at all. But your brain needs the right kinds of nutrients in order to function well, so one way to begin to feel better is to make sure you eat right. Although there is no single food or way of eating that will cure depression, eating the following foods can help.

Complex carbohydrates. Complex carbohydrates, found in whole-grain breads, cereals (oatmeal is an especially good choice), and pasta, as well as fresh fruit, and vegetables, increase serotonin levels in the brain. These higher levels of serotonin decrease anxiety and increase a feeling of calm.

Protein. The protein in chicken, turkey, nuts, eggs, and tuna contains the amino acid tyrosine, which increases levels of dopamine and norepinephrine in the brain and can help you feel energized and alert. Try to eat protein several times a day, but not too close to bedtime, as the increased alertness and energy it provides may make it hard to fall asleep.

Antioxidants. Free radicals are molecules created during normal body functioning, but they can contribute to cell damage and aging. The brain is at particular risk for free radical damage, so eating a diet high in antioxidants, which counter the effects of free radicals, can help to keep your brain functioning well. Antioxidants include beta-carotene (found in cantaloupe, carrots, broccoli, collard greens, peaches, spinach, and sweet potatoes), vitamin C (found in broccoli, grapefruit, blueberries, oranges, kiwi, peppers, strawberries, and tomatoes), and vitamin E (found in nuts and seeds, wheat germ, and vegetable oils).

Omega-3 fatty acids. Omega-3 fatty acids have shown some promise in treating depression. They are found in fatty fish (such as mackerel, tuna, salmon, and sardines), flaxseeds, dark leafy greens, and walnuts. Omega-3s can also be obtained from fish-oil capsules, which can be found in a drugstore or health-food store. In treating depression, omega-3s from fish oil can be more effective than those derived from seed and nut oil, as they enter the brain more readily.

B vitamins. Studies have linked low levels of the B vitamins B_{12} and folic acid to depression. Folic acid is contained in foods such as legumes; dark green, leafy vegetables; many fruits; orange and tomato juice; asparagus; yeast; mushrooms; and organ meats. B_{12} is found in lean animal products such as fish and low-fat dairy products (Fava et al. 1997).

Eat a Balanced Diet

Whether or not you suffer from depression, it's important to eat a balanced diet high in complex carbohydrates, fiber, and nutrients, with some protein and the "good fats"; that is, monounsaturated or polyunsaturated oils and omega-3 fatty acids. This will give you a head start in feeling physically, emotionally, and mentally balanced and healthy.

MOVE YOUR BODY, IMPROVE YOUR MOOD

Regular, moderate exercise has been shown to help alleviate mild to moderate depression (Scully et al. 1998), as well as problems such as anxiety, insomnia, and low self-esteem. As we all know, getting regular exercise helps to keep you physically healthy and fit, which in turn can help you feel better about yourself and your life. Often, however, people with depression feel lethargic and unmotivated to stay physically active, even though exercise can be tremendously helpful in improving depression. Later in this chapter, we'll give you some tips for staying motivated and active.

How Does It Work?

Exercise causes your body to release *endorphins*, which are natural chemicals that help you feel better and more energetic (Yeung 1996). Endorphins reduce the brain's perception of pain. They also act as a sedative, which is why getting regular exercise can help if you're experiencing sleep difficulties. Some researchers believe that exercise may also increase the brain's ability to produce serotonin and dopamine, which are known to help improve mood (Sachar et al. 1980; Nicoloff and Schwenk 1995; Dunn and Dishman 1991).

How Much and What Type of Exercise Do You Need?

All types of exercise can be beneficial for depression. Research has demonstrated that benefits accrue from strength training, aerobic exercise, and flexibility training (Paluska and Schwenk 2000), but any type of regular exercise can help. What's important is for you to get out and move your body, not what type of exercise you do.

Moderate physical activity for as little as ten to thirty minutes a day, three times a week, can be helpful, and in fact, some evidence indicates that moderate-intensity exercise is more effective than high-intensity exercise, possibly because high-intensity exercise may temporarily increase stress (Moses et al. 1989).

Some types of exercise you might consider doing are these:

■ Hiking or walking

■ Dancing

■ Gardening

■ Bicycling

■ Jogging

■ Yoga

■ Swimming

■ Tennis

Choosing an Exercise Activity

When choosing an exercise activity, the most important thing to consider is how much you enjoy doing it. We all know it; if you pick an activity that you don't like, you're far less likely to incorporate it into your lifestyle. Another consideration is how easy it is to include in your existing schedule. You're less likely to keep up with an exercise program if it's difficult for you to get to the gym or to prepare for the activity, or if it's hard to adjust your life to include it. For example, if you decide to join a gym but it's twenty minutes out of your way and always crowded during the only times you can go, you're likely to give up after only a short time.

When deciding on a regular physical activity, ask yourself these questions:

- What do I enjoy doing?

- At what point during my regular day can I add the activity to my life?

- Where would I do this activity?

- How does it fit into my budget and lifestyle?

If you really enjoy getting out in nature to watch birds and wildlife or to look at wildflowers, you might decide to go hiking or walking in your local park several times a week or you might join a hiking club. On the other hand, if you enjoy challenging yourself to beat your previous performance or perfecting a new skill, you might enjoy swimming, bicycling, or tennis more than nature walks. Choose an activity that makes you feel good, not necessarily one that you think would give you the best workout.

Just Doing It

The hardest part about incorporating physical activity into your life is to make it a regular habit, something you do even when you don't necessarily feel like doing it. To turn your new behavior into a habit, you'll need to keep it up for about a month. Often, this will mean doing it even when you'd rather be watching TV after work, rather than going for a bike ride, for example, or walking to the corner store instead of driving. Here are some ways to motivate yourself and to stay motivated to get more exercise.

Decide on a specific goal and create a detailed plan to reach that goal. On a day when you're feeling motivated and energized, sit down and write about a very specific exercise goal that you know you'll be able to reach. For example, if you've decided you'd like to bicycle more, plan to bicycle to and from work at least three times a week. Or you can set a goal to increase the number of miles that you bike: from five miles the first week to ten miles the fourth week, making your goal to bike a little bit further each week, perhaps until you're biking twenty miles a week. Even increasing a one-a-day five-minute walk to ten minutes a day can make a difference. The important thing is not the goal itself, but that you believe you can achieve it and that you'll know it when you reach it. Once you do reach your goal, set some time aside to celebrate, and make sure to set a new goal while you're still excited about your success.

Schedule your exercise time. Use the same calendar, day planner, or handheld device to schedule your exercise sessions that you use to schedule your work and home life, including setting a reminder alarm for yourself. In this way, you'll show yourself that your health is as important to you as all of your other responsibilities are.

Exercise with other people. We often feel more responsibility to others than we do to ourselves, so one way to stick to a new exercise plan is to join other people in exercising. If you're not much of a joiner, you can walk with a friend or your partner three times a week after work. Or if you enjoy being around new people, you can join a class at a local gym, yoga studio, or community center. Search online, in the classified ads, and on community bulletin boards for activity groups that might be seeking new members.

Have a workout buddy. If you know that you tend to lose the motivation to exercise when you're depressed, consider enlisting a responsible, high-energy friend or family member who cares for you to question you regularly about your new exercise plan. You might even want to have this person exercise with you. Exercising together can be a bonding experience and can also make physical activity more enjoyable. But even if your friend or family member doesn't become your exercise partner, ask him or her to remind you to exercise and to encourage you to stick to your new exercise habit.

Vary your routine. It's easy to get bored with an exercise plan if you keep doing the same thing day after day, so remember that all types of physical activity can help improve your mood. Check out the classes in your local community center or community college for ideas about new ways to get physical activity, and during your regular routines look for new ways to increase your physical activity, such as walking instead of driving to lunch, or taking the stairs instead of the elevator.

LIFESTYLE CHANGES CAN IMPROVE MOOD

It may seem simplistic to think that making basic lifestyle changes can improve your mood, but sound sleep, good nutrition, and regular exercise make a big difference for people struggling with depression. There is abundant research that supports this. In the next chapter, we'll talk about how you can use cognitive techniques to counter your negative thought patterns, which also contribute to a depressed mood.

CHAPTER THREE

Using the Mind to Heal Itself

One of the reasons why depression can be so painful is that it causes you to believe your worst fears about yourself and your world. When you're depressed, every interaction with another person can trigger intense self-doubt, and every minor drawback can seem like an insurmountable obstacle. You may find yourself thinking critical thoughts about yourself, assuming the worst about problematic situations and other peoples' intentions, and making generalizations about the way things are for you, such as "I'll always have crappy jobs" or "I'm never going to find anyone to create a meaningful relationship with." When you habitually think this way, it can feel nearly impossible to see your way out of depression; after all, if your own brain is telling you that you're unlovable, stupid, or incompetent, how can you expect to be anything but depressed? Fortunately, there are specific techniques that can help combat such unhealthy thinking patterns.

COGNITIVE BEHAVIORAL THERAPY

Cognitive behavioral therapy (CBT) was developed by Aaron Beck in the 1960s and is supported by a large amount of research as an effective treatment for depression (Butler et al. 2006). As you can tell by the name, CBT looks at cognition, or ways of thinking, in addition to looking at behavior patterns. Beck and his colleagues found that people with depression often make errors in their thinking that fuel their depression, and as a consequence, they behave in ways that contribute to their depression, such as withdrawing from social activities or seeing only the negative aspects of situations. In the throes of this vicious cycle, people who are depressed often cannot see that there are other ways to interact with the world. CBT works by offering alternatives to negative and pessimistic thinking patterns and by supporting positive behaviors that, in turn, combat depressive thinking.

Common Patterns of Depressive Thinking

According to CBT researchers, some of the thinking patterns that can contribute to depression include the following:

■ **Overgeneralization.** Jumping to negative conclusions about situations based on limited information, such as "Nobody at this party likes me."

■ **Black-and-white thinking.** Seeing everything as either bad or good, with nothing in between; for example, "Nothing good ever happens to me."

■ **Catastrophizing.** Anticipating the worst in every situation; for example, "I know I'm not going to get this job."

■ **Discounting the positive.** Downplaying anything positive that does happen, such as "I bet my boss just complimented me because she's buttering me up to do some extra work."

■ **"Should" or "must" statements.** Setting unfair rules for yourself and others, such as "I must always look perfect" or "People should never lose their temper."

■ **Repetitive automatic thoughts.** Having thoughts, often subconscious, that your mind automatically generates in response to familiar situations— thoughts that are often rooted in past experiences or faulty beliefs about yourself. For example, on seeing an attractive man at a party, one type of automatic thought might be "Why bother trying to talk to him? I'm too boring to interest someone like him." Other examples of automatic thoughts might include "I don't deserve to be happy" or "I'm incompetent at everything I try to accomplish."

THE THOUGHT RECORD

This exercise has been used in various forms for three decades, and although it may seem simplistic, it has been shown to be effective in elevating mood in people with depression. If you have difficulty with negative thinking, anxiety, or worry, this exercise can help you learn to step away from your emotions and to look at them more objectively. This is all about keeping a realistic perspective.

Step 1. The next time you feel a particularly unpleasant or intense emotion, stop for a moment and take the time to complete a thought record, rather than just enduring the emotion until it passes.

Step 2. Take a piece of paper and divide it into four columns. Label the first column Mood, the second one Thought, the third one Evidence Supporting the Thought, and the fourth one Evidence Refuting the Thought. In the first column, write down the emotions you're feeling (sad, angry, disappointed, anxious, and so on), then rate the intensity of each emotion on a scale of 0 to 100, where 0 means you aren't experiencing that emotion at all, and 100 means you're feeling it at its most intense extreme. Note that the act of rating your emotion may actually help to alleviate some of the intensity of the pain by itself—no kidding!

Step 3. Ask yourself the following question: "I'm feeling _____ right now; what's going through my mind?" Take a moment to reflect on the thoughts that underlie your emotion. For example, suppose you made a mistake in a presentation and you notice yourself feeling depressed and sad afterward. On reflection, you might realize that you're thinking thoughts like these: "I'm no good at this job. I'm just a loser, and they'll probably fire me over this. I'll never be successful."

In such a case, you might write something like this:

Mood	Thoughts
Sad (75)	*I'll never be a success in this field.*
Depressed (80)	*I'm bad at everything I try.*
Disappointed (50)	*I really messed up that financial stuff in my presentation.*
Anxious (60)	*I bet I'll get fired.*

Step 4. Now assess the truth of these thoughts, honestly and factually. This can be an emotionally intense step, and it may be a challenge to see through your depressive thinking to the real truth of the situation. If you notice yourself automatically thinking, "Yes! That thought is totally true!" consider whether that thought is, in fact, 100 percent accurate or whether the truth is more gray than black or white.

Using the example above, here's how this evaluation might look:

Thoughts	Evidence Supporting the Thought
I'll never be a success in this field.	*There's no evidence to support this.*
I'm bad at everything I try.	*This is simply not true.*
I really messed up that financial stuff.	*I did make an error in the financials; this is true.*
I bet I'll get fired.	*There's no way to know this.*

Step 5. Negative thoughts can feel so real that it may be difficult to see through them. In this step, you'll come up with evidence to refute your negative thoughts. If something is true, then it's true; however, many times our negative thoughts aren't true or can't be proven true. During this step, try to be as objective as possible. If it helps, pretend that you're a lawyer defending your client (you) from your thoughts.

Thoughts	Evidence Refuting the Thought
I'll never be a success in this field.	*I'm on track in my field, based on what I know about*

	the careers of others who have succeeded. It's hard to know if this is true, but the evidence points to this as being false.
I'm bad at everything I try.	*I've made some mistakes, but there are also many things at which I've succeeded.*
I really messed up that financial stuff.	*I did make an error in calculation.*
I bet I'll get fired.	*My supervisor and colleagues were all supportive of me afterward, and they told me the error wasn't a big deal. There's no way to know for sure, but the evidence points to this not being true.*

Step 6. Now look at the evidence in both columns and rate your emotions again. Has the intensity of your emotions lessened? It's normal and healthy to experience sadness, grief, disappointment, and other difficult emotions; however, our thoughts often take our painful emotions and use them as evidence to prove that we are worthless or incompetent. Keeping a thought record like this can help you regain both a realistic perspective and your equilibrium when you are faced with painful or difficult emotions. This is not about sugar-coating reality or fooling yourself into believing

things are okay. It's about seeing reality clearly; the positive and the negative.

If you're seeing a therapist, consider asking him or her to work with you on thought records regularly. As you get better at examining your thoughts more objectively, you may find yourself automatically checking the accuracy of your negative thoughts in everyday situations, without having to write them down.

PREDICTING SATISFACTION

Many people with depression don't anticipate enjoying particular activities, such as going out to a movie with a friend or taking a hike. You may find yourself thinking, "I don't feel like going out. If I go, I'll just be miserable, so why bother?" or "I feel so bad, I know I won't be good company. No one will want to be with me; I'll just stay home." Often, this particular pattern of thought keeps depressed people inactive and isolated.

This exercise, which is a simple reality check, was developed by David Burns (1999). Keep a record of this thought pattern in your journal or notebook over the next two weeks and see what you discover. Here's how it works: list the activities you plan to do for the day in the first column, and then rate your anticipated satisfaction level on a scale of 0 to 100, where 0 means that you doubt you'll take any pleasure or feel any sense of accomplishment in that activity at all, and 100 means that you imagine you'll feel very satisfied at having participated. Then after you've completed the activity, rate your actual level of satisfaction. Your list might look something like this:

Activity	Anticipated Satisfaction	Actual Satisfaction
Washing the car	5	15
Doing the laundry	0	25
Going out to the movies with friends	25	60
Buying the new CD I've been wanting	45	55

Do this for two weeks, and then examine your lists to see if you can detect a pattern. You may find that you got more satisfaction out of doing some activities than you expected to or that there are particular activities, such as socializing with friends, that you tend to want to avoid but that end up actually making you feel better. Armed with this information, you can become more aware of your tendency to withdraw and can then remind yourself that, even if you don't feel like socializing, once you're with your friends, you'll more than likely end up having a good time.

THE TYRANNY OF THE "SHOULDS"

We all do it. We torture ourselves with thoughts of how things "should" be, and we feel bad when things happen that "shouldn't." It's normal human thinking, but it can be an unhealthy pattern that keeps us feeling disappointed, hopeless, and stuck. Here's a simple way to break free from the tyranny of the "shoulds."

The next time you feel upset or sad, create a thought record as explained above, but rather than assessing the truth of your thoughts, rewrite any "should" statements; that is, replace "should" with "I want," and "shouldn't" with "I don't want."

Here's an example of how this works: One day Sara found herself in a familiar mood. She was feeling upset and resentful of her husband for not taking on more of the responsibilities for child care, and for seeming to be distracted and uninterested in his family. While she sat at the kitchen table stewing about her husband, she decided that rather than continue sitting there getting more and more upset, she would try to understand her feelings about the situation. She wrote a thought record that looked like this:

Mood	Thought
Sad (70)	I guess I'm just not interesting to him anymore.
Resentful (95)	Marriage isn't supposed to be this way; it's supposed to be an equal partnership.
Guilty (80)	I shouldn't be so upset. He takes care of us in the ways he knows how.
Angry (55)	He's so selfish; he cares only about himself.

Note that we often think, "This is the way things ought to be" or "Things aren't supposed to be this way," instead of employing the word "should." Notice that there are several "should" statements in Sara's thought record that don't actually use the word "should," but it is implied. So Sara rewrote her first, second, and fourth thoughts this way:

■ *I want him to be more interested in me, the way he used to be.*

■ *I don't want our marriage to be this way.*

■ *I want him to express more care for me and the kids, and I want him to help out more.*

Rather than thinking you shouldn't have a particular thought or that you don't want to feel a certain emotion, it can be much more helpful to acknowledge that you do feel the emotion. So Sara rewrote "I shouldn't be so upset" as "I am upset, and I want things to be different in our marriage so I'll feel cared for and supported."

By doing this exercise, Sara got in touch with her deep need to feel loved and supported by her husband, who had become increasingly distant ever since their kids had been born. Rather than feel angry and resentful at her husband and bad about herself for feeling that way, Sara was able to acknowledge her true feelings and to feel compassion for herself, and she began to think of ways to discuss her feelings with her husband without having to resort to anger and arguments.

MOVING BEYOND SHAME, GUILT, AND SELF-BLAME

Guilt and shame can be healthy human emotions, reminding us that we have a responsibility to treat others with respect. These emotions can point us to areas in which we may need to improve and can mobilize us to accept responsibility for mistakes we've made. But in the midst of depression, guilt and shame can be overwhelming, and people who are depressed often take on much more of the blame for situations than they deserve. Although it's healthy to take responsibility for your actions, too much self-blame and self-criticism will only make you feel bad without solving any of the very real problems that may be present in any given situation. If you feel a lot of self-recrimination and you tend to blame yourself for everything that goes wrong, this next exercise will help you.

Step 1. Sometimes self-blame can be subtle. It may feel like another emotion, or you may not consciously think that you are to blame, while at the same time you feel a deep sadness or grief, which may be rooted in self-blame. Writing down your self-critical thoughts is one of the best ways to understand the nature of self-blame. Begin by answering the following questions in your journal or notebook. You can answer them either in a general way or in terms of a specific problem or issue that you're currently grappling with:

- What do I think of myself?

- What am I telling myself?

- In what ways do I feel as though I am to blame?

- What do I feel shame about?

Step 2. Now divide a page in half and label the two columns Evidence For and Evidence Against. Consider whether there is evidence to support or refute the idea that you are directly and solely responsible for any situations that you may be feeling guilt or shame about. Write down all of the evidence, both supporting and refuting your feelings of responsibility.

Step 3. Look at the evidence in both columns, and for each piece of evidence ask yourself, "Is this 100 percent true?" Focus on the facts, rather than blaming yourself or others.

Step 4. After you do a careful analysis of the facts, if there are clear mistakes you've made and ways in which you've contributed to hurtful situations, consider the following points:

- It can be helpful to own up to any responsibility you may have had and apologize or make other amends, as appropriate. Write down the part of the situation that you do feel responsible for. Rather than beating yourself up over being flawed, though, remember that everyone makes mistakes. If your best friend came to you and confessed that she had behaved in the same way that you had behaved, would you criticize him or her for it, or would you express sympathy and compassion? What would you recommend your friend do to make amends to anyone who might have been hurt?

- Consider your intentions. Most often, we don't mean to cause pain even when we do. Write down your intentions about the situation. For example, if you've said something to a friend that hurt her, you might write, "I knew her behavior was causing her pain, so I honestly wanted to let her know how I view such behavior. I went too far, but my intention was to help her improve herself."

- Give yourself permission to change your guilt into regret. Guilt is so painful because it conveys the message that you are a bad person just because you made a mistake. Regret takes this "badness of self" aspect out of the equation. It's natural and healthy to regret causing another person pain, but making it into a test of your worth as a human being causes even more pain than the original mistake.

- Consider the many times you've been kind, considerate, helpful, sympathetic, and loving. Evaluate these things and then list the situations in your life when you behaved admirably and selflessly, and be sure to list the positive characteristics and attributes that you know you possess. As you review your contribution to the situation that's causing you pain, remember to also keep in mind all of the times that you've been a positive force in the world.

MINDFULNESS

Mindfulness is another cognitive method that has shown promise in improving depression. The technique, originally developed by Buddhist monks, has recently been found effective for many modern problems such as anxiety, chronic pain, and stress. Simply put, *mindfulness* is the act of staying aware of the present moment and of your brain's tendency to spin your experiences into assumptions, stories, and explanations. As you just learned, people with depression often have unhealthy thinking patterns that undermine their sense of self-worth, so mindfulness techniques can help to make you aware of such thoughts. Mindfulness can also help you stay in the moment without getting caught up in judgments, assumptions, and stories about what's happening.

There are many ways to practice mindfulness. One way is to begin a meditation practice, in which you meditate for ten to thirty minutes every day, using various techniques to quiet your mind. There are many books, websites, and CDs available that teach meditation techniques, so we won't go into them in this book.

For those who don't have the time to commit to thirty minutes or more of a daily meditation practice, you can practice mindfulness whenever you think of it, wherever you are. To do the next exercise, try to take about five minutes for it each day. It might help to pick a time and do the exercise at the same time each day. For instance, you might choose to do it just before you go to sleep, immediately after you wake up, at lunchtime when you have some time to sit in a peaceful park, or even in your office with the door closed. You might also consider setting an alarm on a clock, cell phone, computer, or handheld device to remind yourself to meditate. As you become more skilled, you can use the techniques whenever you remember to be mindful, when you feel the need to center yourself, or when you need to calm down.

The important things to remember about mindfulness are that there is no "right" way to be mindful, and you don't have to be mindful all the time to benefit from the meditation practice. Even if you manage only a few mindful minutes a day when you first attempt this, you're doing it successfully. As you continue to practice bringing your mind back to the present moment, you'll find that it becomes easier and easier to do, and you'll notice that being mindful will become almost like second nature.

BE MINDFUL OF THE PRESENT MOMENT

Here's a simple way to center yourself and become mindful of the present moment:

1. Find a quiet place where you can be alone and uninterrupted for at least five minutes. If you wish, set a timer or alarm clock to go off after five minutes, or longer if you'd like to take more time.

2. Sit in a comfortable position with your back supported. Rest your hands on your thighs in a way that feels comfortable.

3. Close your eyes and bring your attention to your breath without changing how you're breathing. Pay attention to your breath as you inhale and exhale and become aware of the sensations of breathing, from the way the breath feels in your nostrils to the way your abdomen rises and falls with each breath.

4. While continuing to be aware of your breath, watch your thoughts as they come into your mind. Rather than clinging to any one thought, just allow them to drift

through your mind like clouds drifting through the sky. As you notice yourself following a thought, gently bring your mind back to your breathing without judgment. Just let the thought go, as if it were a cloud dissipating in the sunlight. This has been referred to as "bare attention"; that is, paying attention without the need to judge or to change your thoughts—just simple awareness.

5. After five minutes or when you feel ready to go back to your day, open your eyes. As you become more comfortable doing this exercise, you can bring your attention to your breath and practice letting your thoughts go at any time, no matter where you are.

Mindfulness can be helpful when used in conjunction with the other cognitive techniques outlined in this chapter. As you become better at watching your thoughts without clinging to them, you'll also get better at seeing the effects your thought patterns have on your moods.

___

More Ways to Be Mindful

Here are some exercises that combine mindfulness skills with cognitive techniques. The important lesson to take from these exercises is that you have the power to decide what to focus on in your life. These tools are designed to help you get better at seeing the world in a balanced way; that is, as neither completely positive nor completely negative.

SITTING WITH SUCCESS

Researchers have found that depressed people often see the world in a more realistic light than people who aren't depressed, because they are exquisitely tuned into the negative aspects of situations (Dobson and Franche 1989). This doesn't mean that the world is entirely a negative place. It does mean that nondepressed people may not see the darker side of things and may not appreciate the complex reality of a specific situation. People with depression, though, usually focus on the negative aspects of life to the extent that their outlook on life becomes unbalanced and everything seems gloomy, threatening, and hopeless to them. If you tend to focus on the darker aspects of life to the exclusion of the positive aspects, here's a way to use mindfulness to balance out your worldview:

Step 1. Find a private, quiet spot where you will be undisturbed for five minutes or more. Sit in a comfortable position. If you wish, have a journal or paper and a pen handy. Close your eyes.

Step 2. Now think back to when you were younger and had plans, hopes, and dreams for the future. Perhaps you remember a time when you were in college and dreamed of owning your own home or of taking a trip around the world. As you remember each of these early aspirations, take note of those goals that you have reached in your life. You might now have a home, a supportive, loving relationship, children whom you love, or a career in the profession you've dreamed about ever since you were a teenager. Perhaps you took that longed-for trip the year you graduated from college.

Step 3. As you become aware of each of the dreams that you've achieved, sit for a moment with the knowledge of what you've accomplished. Simply let the sense of pride, satisfaction, or contentment that you feel rise up in your mind. Savor that feeling. If other thoughts come up, let them go. If you notice yourself trying to discount your successes (with thoughts like "Yeah, but while I was traveling, my friends all had internships and they're all more successful than I am now"), gently let them go. Such thoughts are irrelevant to this exercise.

Step 4. If you wish, write a list of your accomplishments in your journal. As often as you want to, revisit this list or do this exercise, taking the time to be aware of the dreams that you have achieved thus far.

BEAUTY WALK

Often we get so caught up in the stresses of our lives that we forget to look and see the beauty and wonder that's all around us. Everyone does this, not just those with depression, but depressed people are even more prone to discounting their positive moments in favor of the negative. In this exercise, you'll practice being mindful of the joyful, beautiful, mysterious, or just plain silly moments that we all experience every day.

It's easy. Whenever you think of it, stop whatever you're doing (or if you can't physically stop, stop whatever your mind is focusing on in the moment), and become aware of your surroundings or the interactions you're involved in right at that moment. If you wish, you can set an alarm for every few hours, and when it rings, stop whatever you're doing and do this exercise.

To begin, look around you for something positive that you can see, hear, feel, smell, or taste, whether it's a tree's leaves turning autumnal red or a child laughing with his mother as they walk down the street. Maybe you just had a wonderful meal, a friend complimented you on your new haircut, or traffic is flowing much better than you expected. Just notice the moment, savor it, and sit with the feeling for a moment or two. This practice is not meant to be an empty exercise in "turning that frown upside down"; it's meant to help you balance your negative (and sometimes realistic) view of the world with positive input so that you become more balanced in your thinking.

People with depression sometimes scoff at cognitive techniques such as those presented in this chapter, thinking that exercises so seemingly simple couldn't possibly alleviate the misery that is depression. However, a great deal of research has clearly shown that cognitive techniques, when done consistently, can help depressed people gain some distance and objectivity from the negative and distorted thoughts that are often their main symptoms of depression. If you are skeptical about these techniques, that's okay. Nevertheless, we think that if you just try one or two of them and repeat them over several weeks, you'll find yourself understanding with greater clarity how your thought patterns may be contributing to your struggle. This understanding, along with other techniques outlined in this book, can go far in helping you to recover from depression.

CHAPTER FOUR

Enhancing Self-Esteem

Depression saps self-esteem, leaving the person with depression feeling incompetent, unworthy, and unable to see his or her own innate value as a human being. Often, the most painful part of depression is this deep sense of knowing that you are inherently unworthy at your core, and that the people in your life who say that they believe otherwise are obviously misguided. However, as you learned in chapter 3, depression can warp your thought processes so that you believe things that are absolutely untrue.

The good news is that these self-destructive thoughts and thought patterns can be turned around—as long as you are aware of how they operate. This chapter presents simple techniques to help you recognize and remember your own worth and to counteract the effects of the self-deprecating thoughts that are rooted in your depression.

DO YOU HAVE LOW SELF-ESTEEM?

Self-esteem, to put it simply, is a measure of how we feel about ourselves, our sense of our own value as human beings, and our understanding of what we bring to the world. People with low self-esteem struggle with feelings of inferiority and worthlessness, often despite positive feedback from friends, loved ones, and colleagues.

Low self-esteem brings with it strong feelings of inadequacy, indecisiveness, low self-confidence, and unrealistic or overly harsh self-criticism. As you might imagine, low self-esteem and depression frequently go together.

People with high or healthy self-esteem have a generally accurate view of themselves, including a nuanced understanding of both their strengths and weaknesses, and a sense of being generally valuable and worthwhile despite their imperfections, even in the midst of difficult events or circumstances.

We are all influenced by those around us, especially family, friends, and close peers, who often have different values than we do. It's easy to be influenced by the values and beliefs of those closest to us, and to make important life decisions based on what we think others want us to do, rather than what we want for ourselves. Sometimes you may feel bad about yourself because in some way you aren't living by your own values and beliefs.

CLARIFYING YOUR VALUES

In this exercise, we'll help you to clarify your personal values and beliefs, and we'll also help you to explore ways to live more in tune with those values and beliefs. This exercise will help you see that you are not dependent on others' opinions of you. Low self-esteem is often rooted in what we perceive as disdain or even criticism from those who don't share our values, and it can be difficult to separate our inherent worth from the negative feedback of those who wish us to be different.

Step 1. First find a place where you can be undisturbed for at least ten or fifteen minutes. Take a moment to get comfortable. If you wish, you can first do the progressive muscle relaxation exercise or the eye movement exercise from chapter 2, or the meditation from chapter 3. When you feel calm and centered, you can begin.

Step 2. On a sheet of paper, write down the aspects of your character that you feel define who you are, and the values that really matter to you. You might want to include the following:

- Your spiritual values and beliefs

- Social and political issues that matter to you

- The people in your life who mean the most to you

- Values and beliefs you would be willing to defend

- Qualities that you seek in an intimate relationship or close friendship

- Activities that make your life meaningful and enjoyable

- Your favorite places

- Your character and personality traits that other people value

Step 3. As stated earlier, the pressure to conform or to please other people can be at the root of low self-esteem. In old age, however, many people become more philosophical about life and cease to care as much about what others think of them. Those who are growing closer to the end of life often have learned how to put things into perspective, and they care less about the minor irritations and annoyances of everyday life.

For this step, imagine yourself as a very old person—one who knows that life will soon be over. Take the time to get into this persona. Try to really feel what it might be like to be at the end of your life. Then ask yourself these questions: What am I ready to let go of? What obligations can I gratefully release? How does it feel to let go of others' expectations and judgments? What continues to have value for me?

Write down your answers on another sheet of paper or in your journal. How does it feel to finally let go of others' opinions and expectations of you and their notions about who you are and how you should live your life?

Then look back at the list of values that you wrote in step 2. What's still important to you? Which values seem the most significant and worth adhering to from your perspective when you're close to the end of your life?

Step 4. Now that you've become more clear about your deeply held values and you know what matters the most to you, it's important to realize that this is who you are. Those values are the foundation of the real you, and they need to be nurtured and supported in the same way that a living being would be supported and nurtured. This includes the people in your life. You would never allow your young child to spend time with someone who might harm him or her, and you would never give a precious family heirloom to someone you couldn't trust to keep it safe. Neither should you give the care and keeping of your precious self-esteem to people who won't support the real you.

Step 5. At this stage, it will be helpful to create another list with two columns. Label the first column Those Who Support the Real Me, and the second Those Who Don't Support the Real Me. Take an honest look at the people in your life who aren't able to offer support, encouragement, and care to the real you—the you who is reflected in the list you just created about your true beliefs and values—and put them on your Those Who Don't Support the Real Me list. Then write the names of the people who do support and nurture your true self in the Those Who Support the Real Me list.

Consider how you spend your time and with whom. Then ask yourself what kind of changes you need to make in how you live your life so that you receive more support from those who are already supportive, and so you need and expect less from those who cannot offer you acceptance of your true self.

YOUR POSITIVE ACTIVITY DIARY

One way depression drains self-esteem is by convincing you that you don't do anything worthwhile, that your days are spent wasting time. This exercise will help you to see that you have positive experiences every day, that you complete important tasks, and that you are engaged with the world. The diary is simple and you can do it in one of two ways or, if you wish, in both ways.

Option 1. Write down everything you do every day for at least one week. Include even seemingly tiny things, like picking up a coworker's dropped paper or saying good morning to the bus driver.

Option 2. Record only the most significant events of each day for at least a week, including the following categories:

- Tasks completed (or progress made toward completion)

- Positive events (such as giving or receiving a compliment, having lunch with a friend, or seeing and appreciating a beautiful flower on your evening walk)

- Experiences that matter (such as gardening, spending time with a loved one, volunteering, meditating, or saying a prayer)

For both options, keep it simple by just jotting down brief statements in three to five words, rather than describing everything in detail.

At the end of each day, review your list and see whether it's true that you accomplished nothing that day or that you're wasting your days doing nothing. We believe you'll discover that, in fact, you experience many positive, fulfilling moments every day, and you are contributing daily to your own well-being and to that of others.

TIPS FOR ENHANCED SELF-ESTEEM

Here are some strategies you can use to strengthen your self-esteem on a daily basis. Remember that depression has an insidious way of making you believe the worst about yourself and the world. These tips can help you to combat this depressive thinking and to cultivate a more realistic view of the way things are.

Accept compliments. It can be difficult to accept compliments, especially when you're feeling bad about yourself. You might find yourself negating compliments, either out loud or in your head. The next time you receive a compliment from someone, see how it feels to just say thank you, and to allow the compliment sink in. Take a moment to accept as fact that the person really believes what he or she just said to you, regardless of how you might feel about it. Resist the impulse to say (or to think), "Thanks, but…" or "Well, actually, that's not true because…"

Take credit for your accomplishments. When you complete a task, take a moment to congratulate yourself, either aloud or silently. If it's a major accomplishment, such as completing a large project for work or reaching a personal goal you've had for a while, plan a celebration for yourself and your close friends or associates. Be mindful of your tendency to negate your accomplishments or to move on without marking them as significant. How does it feel to celebrate having accomplished something you're pleased with and proud of?

Examine criticism fully. It's common for people with depression to simply accept all criticism, either explicit or implied, while rejecting all compliments. If you find yourself buying into criticism without question, take the time to analyze the critical comment using the skills you learned in chapter 3. Ask yourself, "Is this statement 100 percent accurate? If not, what isn't accurate about it? What's the other side of this criticism?" Also, consider the source of the criticism. If it comes from someone on your Those Who Don't Support the Real Me list, consider that the criticism might be a reaction to you living in line with your own values—values that the critical person doesn't share. Is it possible that the person is trying to cause you shame or pain? If so, how does this affect the validity of the criticism?

Reframe your mistakes. We all make mistakes, both small and large. If you find that you're berating yourself endlessly after every mistake you make, try reframing it. On a separate sheet of paper or in your journal, describe the mistake you made, then explore your mistake by writing about it in these contexts, or simply reflect on these issues in your mind:

- Own the mistake. Take responsibility for it or for your part in it. Be honest with yourself and own only that part of the error that is your direct responsibility.

- Make amends or apologize if you have done something that you regret.

- Consider how you might have behaved differently. Did you have information that could have changed your response or decision? Or given what you knew, did you actually behave in a reasonable way?

- Consider who else might be implicated in the situation. Ask yourself, "Am I really the only one to blame?"

- Ask yourself, "What can I learn from this mistake that can help me not repeat the same mistake in the future?"

Treat yourself as you would a friend. We are often our own worst enemies. If this is true for you, consider changing that by treating yourself as you would a treasured loved one. When you achieve a goal, give yourself a pat on the back; when you're sad, give yourself permission to cry and to reach out for support; when you make a mistake, offer yourself compassion and forgiveness. Make time to enjoy life by doing what you enjoy. Eat well, take care of your health, and remember to take time out to laugh and enjoy your life. Do for yourself what you would advise your best friend to do in your situation.

The mindful moment. Go back to chapter 3 and reread the section on mindfulness, then set aside some time in the day when you know you'll be less busy and you'll have time to stop and savor the moment. It could be the moment you shut down your computer after ending your day's work or during your coffee break in the morning. It doesn't matter what time you do it, only that you take a few minutes out of your day to come back to the present moment, stop, and savor whatever is happening, no matter what it is.

Perhaps you feel tired in that moment. Who wants to savor that? But instead of judging your feeling, stop and feel what this sensation called tiredness is like. How does it feel in your body? What does your mind do with the feeling? See if you can step back for just a moment and experience the feeling in that moment without judgment, condemnation, or a wish that things were different. When you notice yourself judging it ("Ugh, I hate feeling this way! I should have gotten more sleep last night"), just let the thought drift by without attaching any emotion to it. Do this at least once a day, every day, no matter what is happening. We think the more you do this practice, the better you'll become at noticing when your mind is beating you up, judging your situation harshly, or wishing you were anywhere else but where you are.

CHAPTER FIVE

Understanding and Managing Intense Emotions

Depression carries with it some very intense and difficult-to-manage emotions. In addition to the normal difficult emotions that all people experience from time to time, such as anger, sadness, disappointment, and grief, people with depression can also experience seemingly uncontrollable waves of despair, overwhelming anguish, the urge to harm themselves or others, and other intensely negative feelings that, even to the person with depression, may seem out of proportion to the situation. In this chapter, we discuss some ways to manage these overwhelming emotions and to regain your balance when the entire world appears to be confusing or chaotic.

WHAT ARE EMOTIONS?

Emotions can be defined as feeling states that arise unconsciously; that is, we cannot directly control what emotions we may feel at any given time. They usually arise in reaction to a real event or to a mental stimulus, which might be a situation, an interchange between people, a memory, or a thought. Research has proven that emotional states have a profound effect on the body. For example, one study has shown that feeling sincere positive emotions can enhance the immune system, while experiencing negative emotional states may actually suppress the immune system for several hours after the experience that triggered the emotion (Rein, Atkinson, and McCraty 1995).

Many experts think that emotions developed as adaptive mechanisms in humans to aid us in dealing with a variety of experiences, and to signal us to approach positive stimuli that may help us or to avoid negative stimuli that might harm us (Keltner and Haidt 1999.) For example, happiness often makes people outgoing, generous, and more likely to bond with others, while depression signals us to avoid others, to withdraw, and to preserve our energy. Unfortunately, unless we learn to regulate our emotions, some emotions can become overwhelming and may lead us to actions that are harmful, such as lashing out at others, staying in bed all day, or, in some cases, even committing suicide.

Being able to function well while experiencing all sorts of emotions, even the painful ones, is an important skill but many people struggle with regulating their emotions. No one has ever lived without experiencing pain, sadness, grief, and anger, just as no one has ever lived who never felt satisfaction, pleasure, or happiness. Emotions are an integral part of the human experience. But to live well, we must be able to maintain our balance through all sorts of emotions, the painful as well as the wonderful ones.

THE TWO TYPES OF PAIN

Some psychology researchers have described two types of pain. The first type is considered existential pain (Peck 2003), or what one researcher calls "clean pain," which is the normal pain that comes with living an ordinary life (Zettle 2007). This pain comes from such common but nevertheless painful human experiences as losing a loved one; being diagnosed with a serious illness; experiencing abuse, humiliation, or degradation; or perceiving that we have failed at something we hoped would succeed. All humans experience this type of pain to some extent.

The second type of pain is considered neurotic, unnecessary (Peck 2003), or "dirty pain" (Zettle 2007). This pain is pathological, unhealthy, and damaging, and stems from what we tell ourselves about the existential pain we experience. It can also be caused by unrealistic appraisals of ourselves, harsh judgments from others or the world, and a consistently negative view of the world that is unaffected by any positive feedback or events. For people with depression, it is often this unnecessary pain that causes the most suffering.

Sometimes, after a series of disappointments or difficult experiences, normal, existential pain can change into unnecessary pain.

The Importance of Feeling the Pain

Robert Frost once said in a poem, "The best way out is through." It's important to realize that much of our pain is a normal part of life, and that the way through pain is to feel it, rather than hide from it by ignoring it, numbing it through drugs or alcohol, or denying its importance. In fact, the way through depression often involves taking a closer look at your painful experiences, opening up to your pain, and letting go of the thought that you really shouldn't be so depressed. To finally stop struggling against pain and to acknowledge that life can be difficult and painful is to give up the idea that life should be different than it is. This can be a crucial step in recovering from depression.

WRITING THROUGH THE PAIN

Pent-up emotions can contribute to physical health problems like high blood pressure, as well as to depression. In extensive studies, psychologist and researcher James Pennebaker has found this to be true (Pennebaker, Kiecolt-Glaser, and Glaser 1988). He also found that one way to release these pent-up emotions is through *therapeutic writing*, a form of writing that has been shown to improve high blood pressure, strengthen the immune system, and reduce depression (Pennebaker 1997). The technique is surprisingly simple.

Step 1. Pick a time and a place where you won't be disturbed. If you need to first relax and center yourself, consider using some of the techniques we've previously covered in this book, including progressive muscle relaxation, in chapter 2, and mindfulness meditation, in chapter 3.

Step 2. Start writing about an important, difficult, and painful event that's on your mind. This can be a recent event, or it may have happened a long time ago. You can probably think of several such events right now, but write about one that has strong emotional resonance for you. Trust your gut. Usually, the first incident that comes to mind is the one to write about. If you can't think of anything immediately, think back to the most recent time that you felt deep sadness, disappointment, or pain. Write about these experiences as honestly as you can.

Don't worry about sentence structure, coherence, grammar, or spelling; you are the only one you're writing for. The point is to deeply feel the experience again and to write down these feelings. The deeper you go emotionally, the more effective this exercise will be. Write for only twenty minutes. Be sure you stop writing after twenty minutes, even if you have more to say.

Step 3. Repeat steps 1 and 2 once a day for at least four days. Schedule a time to write, and if necessary, set an alarm. It doesn't matter when you write, but it's likely to be helpful to write at the same time every day, when you have twenty undisturbed minutes and can focus on your writing.

Another option is to do this exercise verbally, by speaking into a recording device for twenty minutes, again delving as deeply as possible into the emotional experience, rather than just reporting the facts about what happened. This technique also seems particularly effective in helping people shut off a busy brain that's interfering with sleep.

Pennebaker's research has shown that doing this exercise for only twenty minutes a day for only four days may help you to experience more positive moods, fewer illnesses, and improved immune system function (Pennebaker, Kiecolt-Glaser, and Glaser 1988), which will help you feel better overall, and help you continue to heal from your depression.

QUICK FIXES FOR OVERWHELMING EMOTIONS

At times, everyone experiences emotions so intense that there's no controlling them or talking ourselves out of them. When the emotions you feel are so overwhelming that you just need to stop what you're doing and deal with them, here are some tips for what to do. Remember that feeling your emotions, especially the painful ones, is the way through them. So the next time you feel emotionally out of control, especially if you usually deal with being upset by pretending that nothing's wrong, consider changing your tactics and giving your emotions a few minutes of your undivided attention.

Crying Is Good for You

For years, researchers have been trying to figure out why we cry, but there are still no definitive answers to the question, Why do humans cry at emotional moments? Neurobiologist William Frey has been studying crying since 1983 and has reported something that you probably already know: crying in response to a strong emotion actually can reduce the intensity of that emotion (Levoy 1988). Many people, especially men, believe that it's weak or childish to cry, but in reality, crying is both a natural and a healthy response that may help the body eliminate some of the chemicals that it produces when under stress. Dr. Frey found that tears shed during an emotional crying spell, as opposed to tears caused by nonemotional reasons such as eye irritation, include high levels of stress hormones (Kovach 1982).

You've probably experienced feeling so out of control that you couldn't keep from crying and, after the crying spell ended, feeling calmer and more in control of yourself. But fighting the urge to cry may have the effect of prolonging the painful emotions and of making it more difficult to move through them. So the next time you feel the urge to cry, even if it means you have to take yourself out of the room or away from the situation, do it. When you finish crying, you may feel better almost instantly.

If you have difficulty giving yourself permission to cry under stressful or emotional conditions, consider the following:

- Who told you it isn't okay to cry?

- What reason were you given for this restriction?

- Is it possible that this message is actually incorrect?

- Given what you've just learned about the physical aspects of crying, is it possible that crying is actually a healthy response to stress?

- If it works for you, do it!

Release Tension with Exercise

People who exercise intensely, such as those who do daily runs, often report a runner's high that makes them feel euphoric and eases their pain. This is due to the increase in their serotonin and endorphin levels, which are associated with intense exercise. One way to reduce the stress of overwhelming emotions is to exercise intensely for about ten minutes. You don't have to be an athlete to do this; even a brisk ten-minute walk can help. So the next time you feel upset, consider leaving the situation and going for a quick run or a brisk walk, or doing a whole-body workout to calm down. Make sure you have the right shoes and equipment and that you use caution when exercising, especially if you aren't used to it. If you have any physical problems or chronic conditions, be sure to consult your doctor before beginning any exercise regimen.

TWO-MINUTE REALITY CHECK

The negative effects of overwhelming emotions often have more to do with our reaction to the emotion than to the emotion itself. If you feel extreme rage and act on that rage by breaking a window or physically assaulting the person you're angry at, the problem then becomes the damage you've caused rather than the emotion of anger. If you allow the anger to pass through you without reacting to it, there would be no problem. Emotions themselves, even the painful ones, can be neutral and soon pass. It's when we do things under the influence of strong but temporary emotions that we experience difficulties and then regret what we've done. The two-minute reality check works by interrupting the emotion-reaction cycle, giving you time to regain your perspective.

Step 1. When you find yourself in an emotionally overwhelming situation or dealing with the aftermath of such a situation, ask yourself the following:

- What just happened? What are my feelings, and why do I feel this way?

- In the grand scheme of things, how important is this situation? (Think back to the exercise in the last chapter where you clarified your values by pretending to be a person close to the end of life. What would an elder think of this situation?)

- Given my strong feelings about the situation right now, how upset will I be in twenty-four hours? Forty-eight? A week? A month?

Step 2. Scan your mind for "should/shouldn't" beliefs. You may even want to write them down to clarify your thoughts. What part of the situation are you struggling against? Try reframing your "should/shouldn't" beliefs into "I want/don't want" statements, as you learned to do in chapter 3.

Step 3. If your overwhelming emotion is anxiety or nervousness, try doing two rounds of the eye movement exercise from chapter 2. It may help quite a lot.

Radical Acceptance

Most of the pain of overwhelming emotion is caused by our struggle against feeling the emotion. We fight against our situation, wishing things were different, being disappointed when our expectations aren't met, and telling ourselves we shouldn't be upset, depressed, sad, disappointed, or angry. The next time you feel overwhelmed by intense emotion, try doing the exact opposite of what you normally do: feel the emotion and accept it. Tell yourself, "I'm feeling _____ right now and it is very uncomfortable. I don't have to like it, but it is what I'm feeling in the moment, and I can accept that this is my experience right now. This emotion is only temporary, and it will soon fade."

The energy we expend in fighting off painful emotions actually makes those emotions worse. If you want to explore the feeling of acceptance further, consider starting a regular meditation practice. For more information, go back to chapter 3 and reread the section on mindfulness.

Emotions can be compared to ocean waves. They rise and subside. No one can stop a wave from washing up on the shore, but like surfers, we can learn to ride the waves of emotion without letting them damage us; we can enjoy the swells and stay upright in the troughs, ready for anything. By using the tools found in this chapter, you can learn to recognize your overwhelming emotions for what they are: temporary crashing waves in the greater ocean of your life—waves that have no power beyond what you give to them.

CHAPTER SIX

Staying Connected with Others

Depression often leads people to isolate themselves and keeps them from reaching out and connecting with others. If you're depressed, it may feel scary to be with people; it may feel as if you're opening yourself up to rejection. Or you may feel as though you just don't have the energy to go out and engage in small talk and to laugh at what others laugh at when, internally, you're feeling so awful. You might feel as though you would have to fake it, even to consider going out to be with other people—that you'd be lying to yourself and others. But, not surprisingly, having a consistently active social life can alleviate some of the pain of depression.

Humans are social creatures; we've evolved in ways that enable us to connect with one another. Isolating yourself is a protective impulse that actually can worsen your depression. Please don't misunderstand us: it's healthy to be comfortable with being alone, and it's essential to have some time for yourself, but too much time spent alone—when you're choosing to be alone to avoid being uncomfortable socially—can be unhealthy and may exacerbate depression symptoms.

In the following section, we'll go over ways to motivate yourself to leave the house, whether you want to go or not, by scheduling activities and asking a responsible friend, family member, therapist, or life coach to ensure that you follow your schedule.

We go into quite a bit of detail in this chapter because combatting withdrawal and staying engaged with others have been shown to be especially powerful in overcoming depression.

SCHEDULING PLEASANT ACTIVITIES

The best way to meet and engage with others is to take part in events that are not only social, but also include shared enjoyable activities.

Step 1. Start by listing several things you either have enjoyed doing in the past or have always wanted to do. Or you can choose four to five items from the following list:

Going to a museum, zoo, or amusement park with friends

Joining an activity group, such as a bird-watching club

Taking a class at a local adult school

Visiting the elderly, sick, or shut-ins

Attending a religious service

Camping

Cooking meals with friends

Dining with friends

Going to a movie with friends

Learning a new craft or hobby

Volunteering for a group that helps people or animals

Making food or crafts to sell or give away

Participating in a local community group

Taking a road trip to a scenic area

Spending quality time with your spouse or partner

Going to sporting events

Hiking or walking

Joining a health club

Playing a musical instrument

Playing a sport

Seeing a music or comedy show or other kinds of live performance

Step 2. Now take your calendar, computer, cell phone, or hand-held device (whatever you use to schedule work deadlines or other important items—anything you're likely to see at least once a day), and schedule at least two of the items you wrote down for two days of the upcoming week. For example, you might schedule going out for dinner and a movie in the middle of the week with a few friends, and then arrange to go for a hike with a hiking group the following

Sunday. It will be especially important to plan activities for those times when you would otherwise be alone or socially isolated, such as when your spouse is out of town or a weeknight when you'd normally just watch television. If you have to find the community resources needed to start to engage in your preferred activities, such as finding a hiking group, see the next section in this chapter, Rebuilding Your Social Network.

Step 3. Ask a reliable friend, family member, or your therapist, or hire a life coach to act as your activity coach. Then set up a way for this person to encourage you to follow through with the activities you schedule. Ask your coach to call you the morning or evening before a scheduled activity to see how you feel about going to it, and to call again at the time you'd have to leave to get to the activity on time and to make sure that you go. Make a commitment to yourself to be honest and open with your coach if you're having misgivings or doubts about going.

Step 4. When you schedule your dates, also write a letter to yourself listing your own best reasons to socialize with others, and give the letter to your activity coach for safekeeping.

Step 5. Discuss beforehand the best way to motivate yourself to go to the activity. Should your coach come over and physically pull you out of the house? Or if you refuse to go, should he or she temporarily take away something you value, like your television set? Believe it or not, this approach works. Is there something your coach could say to you that you know will get you out the door? If so, tell it to your coach beforehand.

Step 6. If your coach hears hesitation when talking to you about your upcoming plans, give him or her permission to send or e-mail you the letter you wrote to yourself.

Step 7. Another option is to write out a generous check to a charity or political party you strongly disagree with. Give the check to your coach and agree that if you schedule but fail to attend three activities in a row, your coach will mail your check to the charity or political party. One easy way to ensure you do the activity is to invite your coach to go with you. That way, you are less likely not to attend, and you can talk to your coach throughout the activity if you have anxieties, worries, or distressing thoughts.

Step 8. Go out and do it! If you wish, you can revisit the exercise Predicting Satisfaction, in chapter 3, which asks you to rate an activity on how much enjoyment you think you'll get from it before you go, and then asks you to evaluate how much pleasure you actually did receive from the activity. Most depressed people find they anticipate receiving much less pleasure from engaging in activities than they actually get.

Step 9. Repeat steps 1 through 8 the next week, except schedule four activities during the week, and again arrange with your coach to help you get out to do them. Then, each week, schedule two to four activities for that week. Make filling your weeks with fulfilling activities a project—a scheduling project that you do once a week at the same time of day—and take it as seriously as you would a new fitness regimen. In a short time, you'll find that going out to do things has stopped being a chore and become a habit. Maybe it will even be fun!

REBUILDING YOUR SOCIAL NETWORK

Many depressed people isolate themselves to the point where, if asked how many friends they have, they might say none. A recent study noted that one in four Americans polled said they have no one they feel they can confide in (McPherson, Smith-Lovin, and Brashears 2006). When people have been depressed for a while, they tend to lose friends because they reach out less frequently to them. If you're in this position, you might be wondering how to rebuild your social network. We'll go over some simple ways to do this below.

Just Say Yes

In the movie *Yes Man*, Jim Carrey decides to stop saying no, and to say yes to any proposition that crosses his path. Although we don't recommend saying yes to literally everything, to practice saying yes to every reasonable invitation that comes along is an excellent exercise. This means saying yes to someone who asks you out on a date, even if you're not necessarily interested in that person, or saying yes to a friend who suggests a spur-of-the-moment road trip. It even means saying yes when your hiking group schedules a hike in a beautiful area but you have to get up earlier than you like to do on a weekend. For many depressed people, saying no is almost on autopilot. Over the next few weeks, whenever you feel the knee-jerk reaction to say no, stop for a moment and consider saying yes, just to do something different.

As one saying puts it, "If you do what you've always done, you'll get what you've always gotten."

Ask Your Friends

Our old friends are our best resources to find new friends. For example, dating experts often suggest that you first ask your friends to introduce you to any single people they know, so why not do this for platonic friends, too? It can be awkward to ask friends to help you find more potential friends, but you can ask them if, when they're invited to parties or other events, they could bring you along. Once at the party or event, make a commitment to yourself to speak to at least three people you've never spoken to before. Or if you've previously met most of the people there, commit to speaking to at least three of them before the event is over. If you meet someone you'd like to see again, whether as a friend or as a potential romantic interest, let that person know and give him or her your phone number or e-mail address. The person may not respond, but it's worth a try, and it's good practice in asserting yourself.

Go Online

There are thousands of online social groups whose members have regular face-to-face meetings. Some resources for online interest groups are Meetup.com, Craigslist.org, Facebook.org, Orkut .com, and user-maintained interest groups hosted by Google and Yahoo. Just type "Yahoo groups" or "Google groups" into your web browser and follow the links to find hundreds of groups based on shared interests. For this exercise, find one or two online sources for interest groups, then search for groups of people who share your interests. For example, if you love to see all the new movies, search for "movies." If you'd like to play more tennis, search "tennis."

At first, just so you won't feel overwhelmed, limit yourself to three or four highly active groups, meaning the group has more than one hundred members and they appear to schedule regular, well-attended outings. Then commit to attending the next outing or event that each group organizes. Make sure you attend at least two events before giving up on a group. Sometimes the people who attend may not be suitable (if you're sixty, you may not be comfortable hiking with a group of thirty-year-olds), but it's hard to know that for sure on your first impression. Give each group at least two tries, but if you decide a group isn't right for you, go ahead and look for another one that might be more to your liking.

Volunteer

Volunteer to help others. It can be scary to go to a party or other social event if you're anxious about meeting new people, but when you volunteer, you'll meet people while you're engaged in other activities, and conversation can often flow easier. Moreover, research has shown that helping others can alleviate some of the pain of depression (Musick and Wilson 2007).

To find an opportunity to volunteer, look in your local classifieds in the newspapers, browse the bulletin boards at the local library or grocery store, look in the phone book, or go online. You can visit Craigslist.org and click on "volunteers" under the name of your city, or go to Volunteermatch.org, or just type "volunteer opportunities" and your city or region into your web browser, and see what comes up. You can also call local churches or service organizations in your area and ask if they need any volunteers or if they know of anyone who does. If there are social or political causes that you care strongly about, you can call the headquarters of the political party or a group that does actions on behalf of the cause you're interested in and see if they need help.

ENHANCING YOUR SOCIAL SKILLS

There is often an interpersonal component to depression. You may be feeling so bad that you interact with others in ways that discourage bonding. For example, you may speak softly, avoid looking into the other person's eyes, be uncomfortable with normal physical contact, such as putting your hand on someone's shoulder to indicate sympathy, and be more likely to talk about negative or depressing topics, all of which can send the message that you aren't interested in further interaction with the other person. You may then interpret others' lack of interest or empathy as rejection, which can lead to negative self-criticism, such as "People hate me" or "I can never get along with anyone, so there must be something wrong with me." Thoughts like these, of course, make you feel worse and thus less interested in interacting with others, leading to more "rejections," and on and on. If you find that this is happening in your life, you'll need to interrupt this cycle by paying attention to how you interact with others, and by practicing the type of interpersonal skills that communicate to other people that you are open, interested, and sympathetic and you have a positive outlook.

EXPERIMENT WITH YOUR BODY LANGUAGE

Here's a simple experiment that will help you feel and experience how important body language and facial expression are in personal interactions.

Step 1. For this experiment, you can use a full-length mirror, a sympathetic, trusted friend, or both. Stand in front of the mirror or your friend and imagine that someone has just said (or have your friend say to you), "Good morning. How are you?"

Step 2. Now you'll practice responding twice. If you're using a mirror, pay attention to your facial expression and body language after each response. If you're working with a friend, ask that person to honestly tell you how he or she felt after each of your responses. Did your friend feel drawn to you? Shut out? Confused? Put off?

■ **First response:** Take a deep breath, close your eyes, and imagine a time when you felt happy or content. Take a moment to really get into how that felt for you. How did it feel in your body? Allow your body take whatever position feels right. Try to feel yourself standing tall, squarely facing the mirror or your friend, with your legs planted firmly on the ground, yet relaxed and with your shoulders relaxed. Now open your eyes and respond to "Good morning. How are you?" with whatever words feel right. How did you look in the mirror, and how did your answer feel to you in your body and your mind? Note your facial expression, tone of voice, and how you positioned your body.

■ **Second response:** Now close your eyes and imagine a time (and this may not be difficult) when you felt sad or depressed. Really get into this feeling. Feel it in your body, and let your body position itself in a way that feels as though it fits your mood. You may find yourself slouching a little, turning away from the mirror or your friend, putting your hands into your pockets, or looking at the ground. Now open your eyes and respond to the question in whatever way feels right. Did you notice a difference in how you felt in your body? Did you notice how your facial expression, tone of voice, and body position may have shifted? If you're working with a friend, ask how it was for him or her and what messages he or she got from you based your different responses.

Social Communication in Daily Life

Now take that experiment on the road and simply observe your interactions with others over the next week. Don't try to be different than you are normally; just pay attention, as if you were watching yourself on a video. If you feel particularly brave, ask a friend to go with you to a party or social event and to observe you, too. Then agree to meet afterward, just the two of you, to compare notes.

These are the things to look for:

■ **Eye contact:** How often, in general, did you look into other peoples' eyes when you talked to them? How long did you meet their eyes? What caused you to shift away from eye contact? How did it feel to make eye contact, and when did it start to feel uncomfortable? How long did the other people tend to look into your eyes, and did those people seem comfortable making eye contact with you?

- **Body position:** How did you tend to position your body in relation to other peoples' bodies? Did you face them squarely, with your shoulders and hips both at the same distance from the other person? Or did you observe that you often angled your body fully or partially away from the other person?

- **Hands:** What did you do with your hands when you were interacting with another person? Did you put them into your pockets, play with your hair, touch your face, or let them hang by your sides? How did you feel about what your hands were doing? Did you ever notice feeling nervous about what to do with your hands?

- **Head:** What did you do with your head? Did you completely face the other person, or was your head angled away from him or her? Did you tilt your head? Did you find yourself looking at the ground or at a place lower than the other person's face?

- **Facial expression:** What did you notice about your facial expression? Did you smile most of the time, or did you have a neutral face or a frown? If you smiled, was it real or forced? Did you observe yourself clenching your jaw? How did you feel about your facial expression? Did you ever notice yourself trying to change it in order to seem happier or more relaxed than you really felt?

■ **Voice:** Did people ask you to repeat yourself because you were speaking too softly to be heard?

■ **The meeting:** What did you notice about yourself when you first met others. For example, how did you behave when you arrived at work and ran into a coworker in the hall, or passed a stranger walking toward you on the sidewalk? Did you say hello or make eye contact? Did the other person? What was your response, and what was his or hers? At work, did you notice yourself consciously avoiding having to talk to anyone, or were you eager to begin a conversation? What were your facial expression and body language saying in your first moments of meeting people, and how did they change as the interaction progressed? Were you eager to get out of the interaction and move on?

■ **Conversation:** What did you tend to say in response to others' questions about how you were doing? Did you ask people how they were doing and listen to their answers? How did the conversation flow and what was your part in it? Did you nod as the other person talked and encouraged further conversation with questions? Did you find yourself becoming bored with conversations and wanting them to end? What did you contribute to these conversations, and how did others react to your contributions? Did you feel listened to and respected, or did you feel that the people you were engaging with didn't really care what you were saying or didn't understand you? How often did you feel dismissed by others?

Take some time to talk with a trusted friend or to write in your journal or a notebook about how your social skills may be contributing to your depression. Here are some questions to help you begin:

- Do I tend to discuss or focus on negative, depressing, or somber topics?

- Do I tend to avoid contact with others?

- Do I respond to others with smiles, eye contact, and an interested expression, or do I seem uninterested, bored, or sad when conversing with them?

- Do I face others or angle away from them when in a conversation? Do I lean toward them slightly, or do I lean away?

- Do I ask how others are doing and act interested and open to what they have to say?

- How often do I feel dismissed, disrespected, ignored, or misunderstood by others?

- What do I do when I feel that way?

- In general, how do I feel when I'm interacting with people, both individually and in groups? Comfortable? Anxious? Shy? Irritable? Impatient?

Practice Positive Social Skills

Once you have some idea of how you interact with others, including not only how you physically interact, but what your conversational skills are like and how you feel about interacting with others, you can begin to practice effective social skills. Learning how to communicate effectively will help you build more positive relationships with others, which can then help you to combat depression and negative thought patterns, and help you to feel better about yourself.

In the coming weeks, make it a point to practice the following skills. Think of these skills as if you were practicing a musical instrument or a sport. Note that the word here is "practice," not "perfect," so it's okay to sometimes forget to use these new skills and to make mistakes. If you do make mistakes, note them and become aware of those areas where you need to strengthen your skills. As with sports or playing an instrument, the more often you practice, the better you'll become at skillful communicating and socializing.

Effective Body Language

- Face the other person squarely. Make sure your hips and shoulders are an equal distance away from the person to whom you're speaking.

- Avoid nervously picking at objects, touching your face or hair, or playing with your hair while talking to others.

■ If you're seated, lean slightly toward the other person to indicate your interest, but not so far that you're intruding into the person's personal space.

Vocal Tone

■ Speak loudly enough so that you can be heard, but not so loudly that you overpower others' voices. If you aren't sure how effective your speaking voice is, ask a trusted friend to tell you how your voice comes across. Practice speaking from your diaphragm while standing with your feet squarely on the ground and your legs slightly apart (about the width of your hips). Your legs should be relaxed and your chest expanded, with your shoulders held slightly back.

■ Vary your vocal tone. Try not to speak in a monotone; use a variety of tones and vary the tone of your voice depending on the mood of the conversation.

Facial Expression

■ Relax your face when talking to others. If you tend to clench your jaw, practice relaxing it.

■ Smile when greeting others.

■ Your facial expression should match what you're saying. Practice talking about something terrible you just heard on the news while looking into a mirror, but do this while grinning widely. Do you see the discrepancy? Does it disturb you?

■ Keep your facial expression natural, but notice if you tend to do things like squint your eyes, furrow your eyebrows, bite your lips, or frown while talking to others, and if you notice yourself doing this, stop it. After a while, you'll notice you do it less and less.

■ Practice keeping an open, natural, relaxed facial expression.

Eye Contact

■ Make eye contact with others when speaking to them, but don't stare. Although there's no rule about how long to maintain eye contact, we recommend breaking the contact after about five to eight seconds. Then look away briefly and then make eye contact again.

Conversation Skills

■ People like it when you're interested in them, so stay interested in the person with whom you're conversing. You can keep a conversation going by asking sincerely interested questions about what the other person is saying.

■ Self-disclosure can help people to relax and bond, so when appropriate, be sure to talk about yourself, too, with the two following caveats:

　　■ Don't hijack the conversation. Be sure not to turn every conversation around to your experience. If someone is relating an experience to you, rather than saying, "Oh, yeah, that happened to me, too," and then launching into your story, allow others to finish their stories, and then ask questions about their experience.

■ Keep disclosure appropriate. Make sure you disclose only appropriate information and only at appropriate times. This is basic common sense: Don't talk about your sex life in a business meeting, don't disclose your mother's suicide to a casual acquaintance when you've been talking about the weather, and don't bore a table full of people with your entire life story. Make it a point to check the body language of the people you're with to be sure they're interested and listening. If they're not, it's time to give the floor to someone else.

Entire books have been written about the best way to communicate with others, and we've touched on this topic only briefly. If you feel you need more help with learning how to interact effectively with others, we recommend *The Interpersonal Solution to Depression*, by Jeremy W. Pettit and Thomas Ellis Joiner (2005) or *Messages: The Communication Skills Book*, by Mathew McKay, Martha Davis, and Patrick Fanning (2009).

CHAPTER SEVEN

Preventing Relapse

Research shows that your chances of experiencing depression again increase with each depressive episode (Demitrack 2005). That is, the more often you experience depressive episodes, the more likely you are to experience another. Fortunately, research also shows that recovery from depression is possible, and very likely, if you continue to keep up the new habits you've formed to counter the depression and, if necessary, continue the professional treatment you've found for your depression (National Institute for Mental Health 2009).

WHAT RESEARCH TEACHES US

Studies have demonstrated that the people with the highest risk of relapsing into depression are those who have aggressive personality traits and those who have low dependency on others (Gollan and Jacobsen 1999); possibly this is because both groups have low levels of social support. The same study found that people who relapse reported lower levels of satisfaction and pleasure from their activities than people who didn't experience a relapse.

Another study has shown that people who have recovered from depression experience more sensitivity to their low moods than people who have never been depressed, and that even mild low mood or sadness may trigger a relapse (Segal et al. 2006). This study suggests that people who have been depressed need to learn the skills to recognize their dysfunctional thinking patterns in order to prevent themselves from sinking into depression when sadness or other difficult emotions arise. These studies show us that susceptibility to depression is often based on personality style, and that people with particular personality styles need to remain alert to any signs that depression may be taking hold again. Luckily, it's possible to prevent relapse, and to head off a full-blown episode of depression, even when relapse seems imminent.

Recent large-scale studies have shown that when depression is treated with antidepressants, the goal is full recovery (total elimination of symptoms) rather than a partial response (Rush et al. 2006). Many people who take antidepressants experience significant improvement, but not a total recovery. Those who fully recover have a much better chance of avoiding relapse than those who recover only partially. What this means, in practical terms, is that if you're being treated with medications, don't settle for partial improvement. Work with your doctor to try to achieve full recovery. Those who fully recover may certainly have subsequent episodes of depression, but the risk of future episodes is reduced when treatment is sufficient to achieve full recovery.

THE KEYS TO PREVENT RELAPSE: SLEEP AND EXERCISE

In the research on depression relapse, two things have become apparent: maintaining a balanced circadian rhythm helps to keep your mood stable, and so does getting regular exercise. A *circadian rhythm* is an approximate daily periodicity, a roughly twenty-four-hour cycle in the biochemical, physiological, and behavioral processes of living beings. What this means is that if you do two things to stay well—get enough sleep and enough exercise—your chances of relapsing diminish considerably.

Keep a Regular Sleep Schedule

Getting seven to nine hours of sleep every night has been shown to protect against depression (Ehlers et al. 1993; Power 2004), as does maintaining your natural circadian rhythm; that is, your sleep-wake schedule. The best way to keep a balanced sleep schedule is to wake up at the same time every morning, even on weekends. It has also been shown that getting five to ten minutes of light as soon as you wake up can boost your mood (Leppamaki et al. 2002). This form of light exposure doesn't require intense light (as is needed to treat seasonal affective disorder); it can be achieved by turning on a lamp next to your bed with a 100-watt lightbulb. The key to aiding the stabilization of your circadian rhythm is that the light exposure occurs at the same time each day.

Some people use a lamp plugged into a timer that turns on at the same time each day. If you live in an area that has a high number of overcast days, you may want to invest in a high-intensity light box, which is available for purchase on the Internet. However, it is very important that people who suffer from bipolar disorder not use high-intensity light exposure without medical supervision. In bipolar disorder, excessive intense light can cause manic episodes.

Get Regular Exercise

Research has shown that people who take ten thousand steps a day are less likely to relapse into depression (Thayer et al. 2003). This book has already encouraged you to develop regular exercise habits; however, to ensure that you take ten thousand steps a day, you can buy a pedometer at any sporting goods store or online. Simple ways to increase the number of steps you take daily include using the stairs instead of the escalator or elevator, parking farther away from your destination and walking, and, whenever possible, walking instead of driving.

KEEP DOING WHAT YOU'RE DOING

The most important way to ensure that you stay free of depression is to continue to do what works, especially after you start feeling better. If you're taking antidepressant medications, continue to do so even when you feel that the depression has lifted. This most likely means that the medications are working. If you feel you want to stop taking the medication, discuss it with your medical provider. Standard treatment guidelines for medication use in depression suggest that once symptoms are completely resolved, you should continue to take antidepressants for a minimum of six months, at the same dose. The continued treatment significantly reduces the likelihood of an acute relapse. After the additional six months of treatment, most people can gradually discontinue taking their medications without serious risk of acute relapse. However, when tapering off antidepressants, it's essential to do so under medical supervision.

Similarly, if you've read through this book and implemented the suggestions we've made, continue your regimen once your depression has lifted. Keep exercising, eating well, getting enough sleep, practicing your cognitive skills, using mindfulness to stay in the moment, and staying socially active.

Recovering and staying free from depression is like going on a diet. You can't go back to your old habits once you've lost the weight. Staying well—like staying at a healthy weight—often means changing your lifestyle for good. Luckily, not only are all of the skills and tips in this book good for depression, they're also good for your body and soul. With the possible exception of some temporary side effects from antidepressant medication, nothing recommended in this book will make you feel worse. So once you've found some techniques that work for you, consider cultivating them as lifelong habits. You'll be less likely to experience depression and more likely to recover quickly should another episode occur.

HOW TO STAY MOTIVATED

Of course, we all know how easy it is to slip back into old habits. Once you start feeling better, you may feel so good that you forget to practice mindfulness every day; you may discontinue the habit

117

of catching and checking the accuracy of your thoughts; you may skip healthy meals for quick, tasty snacks; you may run out of your mood supplements; and you may find yourself canceling your therapy appointments because you feel as if you just don't need them anymore. Here is a way to make sure you stick to your healthy habits, even when you feel that you are free and clear of depression.

Connecting with Others

One good way to stay on track is to have a person, or even several people, who care about you maintaining your health and who will check in with you occasionally to make sure that you continue to stay healthy. This could be a trusted friend, family member, romantic partner, therapist, doctor, or one or more group members if you belong to a support group of any kind. Make it a habit to check in regularly, either at the start of a session if the person is your therapist, or at monthly or even weekly intervals in conversations or phone calls. Make an agreement with this person that if he or she sees you starting to slip back into your old habits, to encourage you to continue nurturing your good health. Ask the person to help you stick to your new healthy lifestyle, and agree to help this person stay on track with his or her goals, in return.

RELAPSE TRIGGERS

Relapse is possible, but staying vigilant to the signs and symptoms of relapse is also possible and can help to prevent a relapse. Everyone's depression triggers are different, so you'll need to explore your particular triggers and habitual reactions and become familiar with them to make sure that if you start drifting into depression, you will be able to catch it before it becomes a full-blown episode.

Your relapse triggers. For this exercise, get some sheets of paper or your journal, then think back to all of the depressive episodes that you remember and make a list of them. What happened to trigger your depression? You may have had relationship problems, job losses, or money difficulties. Some people find that their depression triggers always share a common theme. For example, you may find that you slip into depression whenever you feel rejected or whenever you feel that you've failed at something important to you. One woman realized that she became profoundly depressed whenever a relationship ended, even if she knew in her heart that the man wasn't good for her. Even the ending of bad relationships made her depressed. Do you see any themes or patterns in your past depressions?

Your depression reactions. Now think back to everything that was happening to you before you became depressed and to how you reacted when depressed. Did you become withdrawn and less social? Did you eat less and sleep more? Or did you turn to alcohol or drugs? Write down every detail you can remember about your descent into depression. When you finish, see if you can pick out any patterns.

For example, perhaps you'll notice that when your mood starts becoming low, you have a harder time getting up in the morning to go to work, you awaken later and later in the day, and you call in sick more often. Or you realize that each time you've been depressed, you felt less and less like socializing, and you watched more television. You might notice that you started ruminating more at work and got less work done, or that you started eating more junk food.

Write down all the signs you can remember from your previous experiences with depression. These are things to watch out for in the future that might indicate a possible relapse.

Get Your Loved Ones Involved

Once you know what to look for, it's time to get your friends, family, spouse, or partner involved in helping you stay well. Often the people closest to us notice a change in behavior before we do, and in the case of depression, the sooner you nip it in the bud, the more likely you are to avoid another depressive episode. Sit down with the person you chose to help you monitor your depression and share your list of depressive behaviors. Point out that these are the signs that you may be becoming depressed again, and explain that if he or she notices any of these signs, to bring that to your attention immediately. If your support person has noticed any possible signs of depression, think of an action plan together. Most people with depression wait too long to get help, thinking that it will just go away or that they can handle it on their own, but before they know it, they are spiraling into clinical depression. Before you get that far, make sure your support person knows what to do.

1. If any of your known triggers of depression have occurred lately in your life, such as a marital or romantic breakup or other major disappointment, or you're feeling rejected or as though you've failed at something, take it as a sign that you need to be extra alert to possible signs of depression. Let your support person know that you need him or her to stay alert, as well.

2. At the first sign of any of the symptoms on your list, your support person should express concern that you're becoming depressed. Think of a phrase or an approach that you know won't upset you when you're feeling down. For example, perhaps the sentence "I'm really concerned that you are feeling sad again" would be more effective than a flip "You're not getting depressed again, are you?" Give some thought to how your support person can approach you without making you feel defensive.

3. Once your support person has brought it to your attention that you may be heading toward depression again, if you don't respond by seeking help, then agree to a time frame in which he or she has your permission to seek help on your behalf. One possible time frame might be two weeks. Show your support person where you keep the phone number of your therapist if you have one, and that of any medical professional who treated your depression in the past. Then give your support person permission to make an appointment for you and to tell your therapist that you may be becoming depressed again.

4. Be sure your support person agrees to remind you to go to your appointment. Then follow your doctor's treatment advice, and be sure to go to any follow-up appointments.

5. Write down your agreement with your support person, and make sure you both have signed and

dated copies. When you begin to feel depressed, you may "forget" that you had an agreement or you may feel that it isn't important anymore. Having a copy of the agreement will remind you that you agreed to honor it, and you may be more inclined to honor it when you see the agreement on paper.

SETTING PERSONAL GOALS

One way to remind yourself to stay on track with your recovery goals is to write down your personal goals and post them where you'll see them every day. Use places like your bathroom mirror, your refrigerator door, or somewhere near your computer screen at work.

Once you've found some techniques that work to alleviate your depression, write a list of your new habits and set goals for how often you want to do them. For example, if you find that taking your medications regularly, seeing a therapist once a week, staying socially active, and exercising regularly all make you feel better, you might write a list that looks like this:

1. *Take my medications every day, as prescribed.*

2. *See my therapist once a week. If I have to cancel, reschedule immediately.*

3. *Plan to go out with friends or to a group event twice a week. (Plan this each Monday during my scheduling session.)*

4. *Hike or walk at least two hours each weekend, plus bike for at least an hour, three days a week, after work. Schedule these on my iPhone.*

Then post the list, or even multiple copies of it, where you'll see it every day. If you're working with a support person, you might also give that person a copy and ask him or her to question you regularly about how meeting your weekly goals is going.

SEEKING BALANCE

Everyone is different, and we all have different needs in terms of how socially active we are, what challenges us, and what is pleasurable or unpleasant for us. In short, nobody can tell you what combination of work, activity, socializing, alone time, and entertainment is best for you.

A good example of normal human variation can be found in the difference between introverts and extroverts. Introverts tend to just naturally enjoy more alone time and to need more time to recover between social events. It's not that they dislike people or socializing, they may just need to recharge. On the other hand, extroverts thrive on being around people and having constant interpersonal interactions. They are more likely to dislike being alone, and they feel more energized after social events compared to before them. These personality types are both normal; they're just different.

Because we're all so different, you'll need to find what works in your life in terms of how you spend your time. You might naturally enjoy more alone time than some of your friends, and they may express concern for you if you choose to stay home one night, rather than go to a movie with them.

The important thing is that you find balance in your life between productive activities, relaxation, intellectual challenges, and just plain fun. Living in balance is likely to help you stay well because you'll be getting many of your needs met: the need for mental challenges, the need to relax and enjoy time with your loved ones, the need to be productive, and the need to let go of all rules and responsibilities and just live in the moment.

If you start to feel out of balance, that is, stressed, unhappy, sad, confused, or frustrated with a particular part of your life, this is a sign that your life might be slipping out of balance. If you notice uncomfortable symptoms such as these, it might be a good time to sit down and consider whether there's anything in your life that needs attention. Look carefully at the following categories and consider whether there's anything you need that you're not getting:

- **Health.** Are you at a healthy weight, free of pain or discomfort most of the time, and functioning well physically? Do you get enough exercise? If you have any health problems that need to be addressed, have you addressed them?

- **Family.** Are most of your family relationships emotionally healthy? Are you able to communicate with family members when there are problems? Do you generally feel supported by your family? If there are any problems with your family that need to be addressed, such as alcoholism, mental health issues, health problems, or child behavior problems, are they being addressed?

- **Social life.** Do you have one or more close friends whom you feel you can confide in? Do you feel that you generally can connect with people? Do you attend social events regularly? Do you feel that you get along well with others and enjoy their company? Do you have meaningful relationships, including a romantic partner if that's important to you? Is your relationship with a partner or spouse generally healthy, and do you feel as though you get your most important needs met most of the time?

- **Work.** Do you feel that you have something productive to do every day? At the end of the day, do you feel that you leave your work at your workplace more often than not? Are your relationships with your coworkers and managers basically sound? Do you feel challenged in your job yet not overly stressed? Do you find your work fulfilling at least part of the time?

- **Spirituality.** Do you regularly find time to quietly contemplate your life and your place in the universe, and to center yourself? Are you connected to a community that shares your spiritual or religious beliefs? If it's important to you, do you attend religious services regularly?

- **Creativity and leisure time.** Do you regularly find the time to be creative in whatever way you choose to be? Do you have hobbies or interests that take you out of your logical mind for a while? Do you take the time to relax, enjoy the good things in life, or learn new skills?

If you answered yes to most of the questions above, your life is probably fairly well-balanced. But if you notice areas for which you answered no, you may want to think about whether you need to do some work in that area to gain more balance. If, for example, you realize that you have very little time to engage in a contemplative practice, whether it is meditation, walking in beautiful places, attending religious services, or praying, you might consider taking an hour or two a week to attend to your spiritual life in whatever way is meaningful to you.

Similarly, if you realize that your relationship with your mother isn't as healthy as you'd like it to be and that this is causing you to feel some emotional stress, you might want to think of ways to help the relationship, either by working on it with your therapist, attending family counseling with your mother, or having a long-delayed conversation with her to try to clear the air.

IN CONCLUSION

Recovery from depression is possible. People get well every day and stay well, often for the rest of their lives. Obviously, although we can't predict whether you'll be free from depression forever, the skills you learned in this book will help to keep you healthy in body and mind. The important thing to bear in mind with depression, as with anything, is to feel compassion for yourself in your heart. Your depression, although painful and sometimes frightening, is a sign that aspects of your life need attention. By buying and reading this book, you've taken the most important first step for recovering from depression and building a healthy life for yourself: you've decided to take action. Congratulations! We wish you the best of luck in staying happy and healthy in the future.

Medical Disorders That Can Cause Depression

- Addison's disease
- AIDS
- Anemia
- Asthma

- Chronic fatigue syndrome

- Chronic infection (mononucleosis, tuberculosis)

- Chronic pain

- Congestive heart failure

- Cushing's disease

- Diabetes

- Hypothyroidism

- Infectious hepatitis

- Influenza

- Malignancies (cancer)

- Malnutrition

- Multiple sclerosis

- Parkinson's disease

- Porphyria

- Premenstrual dysphoria

- Rheumatoid arthritis

- Sleep apnea

- Syphilis

- Systemic lupus erythematosus

- Ulcerative colitis

- Uremia

Drugs That Can Cause Depression

Type	Generic name	Brand name
Alcohol	Wine, beer, spirits	Various
Stimulants	Methamphetamine, cocaine	
Antianxiety drugs	Diazepam Lorazepam Alprazolam	Valium Ativan Xanax
Antihypertensives (for high blood pressure)	Reserpine Propranolol hydrochloride Methyldopa Guanethidine sulfate Clonidine hydrochloride Hydralazine hydrochloride	Serpasil, Ser-Ap-Es Inderal Aldomet Ismelin sulfate Catapres Apresoline hydrochloride
Antiparkinsonian drugs	Levodopa/cardidopa Levodopa Amantadine hydrochloride	Sinemet Dopar, Larodopa Symmetrel

Interferon	Interferon	Multiferon, Roferon A, Reliferon, Avonex Rebif, Betaferon
	Pegylated interferon	Pegasys, PEG-Intron
Birth control pills	Progestin-estrogen combination	Various brands
Corticosteroids and other hormones	Cortisone acetate Estrogen	Cortone Premarin, Ogen, Estrace, Estraderm
	Progesterone and derivates	Provera, Depo-Provera, Norlutate, Norplant, Progestasert

Often when people are treated with a number of prescription drugs, there can be drug-drug interactions that cause depression. If you are taking a number of prescription drugs and experiencing depression, please speak to your physician or pharmacist about the possibility that drug interactions may be causing or contributing to your depression.

References

Agency for Health Care Policy and Research. 1999. Treatment of depression—newer pharmacotherapies. Summary, Evidence Report/Technology Assessment: Numnber 7, March 1999. www.ahrq.gov/clinic/epcsums/deprsumm.htm.

American Psychiatric Association (APA). 2000. *Diagnostic and Statistical Manual of Mental Disorders*, 4th ed., text revision. Washington, DC: American Psychiatric Association.

Avis, H. 1993. *Drugs and Life*. Dubuque, IA: W. C. Brown and Benchmark.

Burns, D. 1999. *Feeling Good: The New Mood Therapy*. New York: Harper.

Butler, A. C., J. E. Chapman, E. M. Forman, and A. T. Beck. 2006. The empirical status of cognitive-behavioral therapy: A review of meta-analyses. *Clinical Psychology Review* 26(1):17-31.

Clayton, A. H., J. F. Pradko, H. A. Croft, C. B. Montano, R. A. Ledbetter, C. Bolden-Watson, K. I. Bass, R. M. Donahue, B. D. Jamerson, and A. Metz. 2002. Prevalence of sexual dysfunction among newer antidepressants. *Journal of Clinical Psychiatry* 63(4):357-366.

Demitrack, M. A. 2005. Difficult-to-treat depression: Better choices, better outcomes. Program and abstracts of the American Psychiatric Association. 158th Annual Meeting in Atlanta, Georgia, May 21-26.

DeRubeis, R., S. Hollon, J. Amsterdam, R. Shelton, P. Young, R. Salomon, J. O'Reardon et al. 2005. Cognitive therapy vs. medications in the treatment of moderate to severe depression. *Archives of General Psychiatry* 6(4):409-416.

Dobson, K., and R. L. Franche. 1989. A conceptual and empirical review of the depressive realism hypothesis. *Canadian Journal of Behavioural Science* 21(4):419-433.

Dunn, A. L., and R. K. Dishman. 1991. Exercise and the neurobiology of depression. *Exercise and Sport Sciences Reviews* 19:41-98.

Ehlers, C. L., D. J. Kupfer, E. Frank, and T. H. Monk. 1993. Biological rhythms and depression: The role of zeitgebers and zeitstorers. *Depression* 1(6):285-293.

Fava M., J. S. Borus, J. E. Alpert, A. A. Nierenberg, J. F. Rosenbaum, and T. Bottiglieri. 1997. Folate, vitamin B_{12}, and homocysteine in major depressive disorder. *American Journal of Psychiatry* 154(3):426-428.

Flora, S. R. 2007. *Taking America Off Drugs: Why Behavioral Therapy Is More Effective for Treating ADHD, OCD, Depression, and Other Psychological Problems.* Albany, NY: SUNY Press.

Ford, D. E., and D. B. Kamerow. 1989. Epidemiologic study of sleep disturbances and psychiatric disorders. An opportunity for prevention? *Journal of the American Medical Assoociation* 262(11):1479-1484.

Frey, W. H. 1983. Crying behavior in the human adult. *Integrative Psychiatry* 1(3):94-101.

Gollan, J., and N. Jacobsen. 1999. Personality styles predict those at risk for recurring major depression. Press release: University of Washington, November 12, 1999. www.washington.edu/newsroom/news/1999archive/11-99archive/k111299b.html.

Goodwin, F. K., and K. R. Jamison. 2007. *Manic-Depressive Illness,* 2nd ed. Oxford, United Kingdom: Oxford University Press.

Keltner, D., and J. Haidt. 1999. Social functions of emotions at four levels of analysis. *Cognition and Emotion* 13(5):505-521.

Kovach, T. 1982. Tear toxins. *Omni,* December.

Leppamaki, S. J., T. T. Partonen, J. Hurme, J. K. Haukka, and J. K. Lonnqvist. 2002. Randomized trial of the efficacy of bright-light exposure and aerobic exercise on depressive symptoms and serum lipids. *Journal of Clinical Psychiatry* 63(4):316-321.

Levoy, G. 1988. Tears that speak. *Psychology Today,* July–August, 8-10.

Linde, K., G. Ramirez, C. D. Mulrow, A. Pauls, W. Weidenhammer, and D. Melchart. 2009 (updated). Why do people use botanicals? St.-John's-wort for clinical depression: An overview and meta-analysis of randomised clinical trials. *British Medical Journal* 313(7052):253-258.

Lu, S. C. 2000. S-adenosylmethionine. *International Journal of Biochemistry and Cell Biology* 32(4):391-395.

McKay, M., M. Davis, and P. Fanning. 2009. *Messages: The Communication Skills Book,* 3rd ed. Oakland, CA: New Harbinger Publications.

McPherson, M., L. Smith-Lovin, and M. E. Brashears. 2006. Social isolation in America: Changes in core discussion networks over two decades. *American Sociological Review* 71(June):353-375.

Moses, J., A. Steptoe, A. Matthews, and S. Edwards. 1989. The effects of exercise training on mental well-being in the normal population: A controlled trial. *Journal of Psychosomatic Research* 33(1):47-61.

Musick, M., and J. Wilson. 2007. *Volunteers: A Social Profile.* Bloomington, IN: Indiana University Press.

National Institute of Mental Health. 2009. www.nimh.gov.

Nicoloff, G., and T. S. Schwenk. 1995. Using exercise to ward off depression. *Physician and Sportsmedicine* 23(9):44-58.

Paluska, S. A., and T. L. Schwenk. 2000. Physical activity and mental health: Current concepts. *Sports Medicine* 29(3):167-180.

Pampallona, S., P. Bollini, G. Tibaldi, B. Kupelnick, and C. Munizza. 2004. Combined pharmacotherapy and psychological treatment for depression: A systematic review. *Archives of General Psychiatry* 61(7):714-719.

Papakostas, G. I., J. E. Alpert, and M. Fava. M. 2003. S-adenosyl-methionine in depression: A comprehensive review of the literature. *Current Psychiatry Reports* 5(6):460-466.

Peck, M. S. 2003. *The Road Less Traveled.* New York: Touchstone Editions.

Peet, M., and D. F. Horrobin. 2002. A dose-ranging study of the effects of ethyl-eicosapentaenoate in patients with ongoing depression despite apparently adequate treatment with standardized drugs. *Archives of General Psychiatry* 59(10):913-919.

Pennebaker, J. W. 1997. *Opening Up.* New York: Guilford.

Pennebaker, J. W., J. K. Kiecolt-Glaser, and R. Glaser. 1988. Disclosure of traumas and immune function: Health implications for psychotherapy. *Journal of Consulting and Clinical Psychology* 56(2):239-245.

Pettit, J. W., and T. E. Joiner. 2005. *The Interpersonal Solution to Depression: A Workbook for Changing How You Feel by Changing How You Relate.* Oakland, CA: New Harbinger Publications.

Poldinger, W., B. Calanchini, and W. Schwarz. 1991. A functional-dimensional approach to depression: Serotonin deficiency as a target syndrome in a comparison of 5-hydroxytryptophan and fluvoxamine. *Psychopathology* 24(2):53-81.

Power, M., ed. 2004. *Mood Disorders: A Handbook of Science and Practice*. West Sussex, England: John Wiley and Sons.

Preston, J. D., J. H. O'Neal, and M. C. Talaga. 2008. *Handbook of Clinical Psychopharmacology for Therapists*, 5th ed. Oakland, CA: New Harbinger Publicaitons.

Rein, G., M. Atkinson, and R. McCraty. 1995. The physiological and psychological effects of compassion and anger. *Journal of Advancement in Medicine* 8(2):87-105.

Rush, J., M. H. Trivedi, S. R. Wisniewski, A. A. Nierenberg, J. W. Stewart, D. Warden, G. Niederche, et al. 2006. Acute and longer-term outcomes in depressed outpatients requiring one or several treatment steps: A STAR*D report. *American Journal of Psychiatry* 163(11):1905-1917.

Sachar, E. J., G. Asnis, U. Halbreich, R. S. Nathan, and E. F. Halpern. 1980. Recent studies in the neuroendocrinology of major depressive disorders. *Psychiatric Clinics of North America* 3(2):313-326.

Scully, D., J. Kremer, M. M. Meade, R. Graham, and K. Dudgeon. 1998. Physical exercise and psychological well-being: A critical review. *British Journal of Sports Medicine* 32(2):111-120.

Segal, Z. C., S. Kennedy, M. Gemar, K. Hood, R. Pedersen, and T. Buis. 2006. Cognitive reactivity to sad mood provocation and the prediction of depressive relapse. *Archives of General Psychiatry* 63(7):749-755.

Su K. P., S. Y. Huang, C. Tsan-Hung, K. C. Cherh Huang, C. L. Huang, H. C. Chang, and C. M. Pariante. 2008. Omega-3 fatty acids for major depression during pregnancy: Results from a randomized, double-blind, placebo-controlled trial. *Journal of Clinical Psychiatry*, 69(4):644-651.

Thayer, R., O. Godes, N. E. Lobato, M. Serrano, J. Hernandez, and S. Culver. 2003. Walking, energy, and mood are interrelated: An important health indication. Paper presented at the American Psychological Association Annual Meeting in Toronto, Canada, August, 2003.

Yeung R. R. 1996. The acute effects of exercise on mood state. *Journal of Psychosomatic Research* 40(2):123-141.

Young, A. S., R. Klap, C. D. Sherbourne, and K. B. Wells. 2001. The quality of care for depressive and anxiety disorders in the United States. *Archives of General Psychiatry* 58(1):55-61.

Zettle, R. 2007. *ACT for Depression: A Clinician's Guide to Using Acceptance and Commitment Therapy in Treating Depression.* Oakland, CA: New Harbinger Publications.

Zisook, S. 1993. Aging and bereavement. *Journal of Geriatric Psychiatry and Neurology* 6(3):137-143.

John D. Preston, Psy.D., ABPP, is professor emeritus at Alliant International University in Sacramento, CA. He is author of twenty books and the "Drugs in Psychiatry" chapter in *The Encyclopedia Americana*. He lectures internationally.

Melissa Kirk is a writer and editor living in the San Francisco Bay Area who has personal experience with depression and has successfully used many of the techniques in this book.

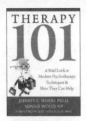
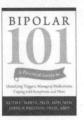

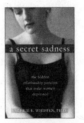